W9-CDK-024

Life Among the Samurai

Among the

Titles in The Way People Live series include:

THE WAY
PEOPLE
LIVE

Life Among the Samurai

by Eleanor J. Hall

Lucent Books, P.O. Box 289011, San Diego, CA 92198-9011

Library of Congress Cataloging-in-Publication Data

Hall, Eleanor J.
    Life among the samurai / by Eleanor J. Hall.
      p.   cm. — (The way people live)
    Includes bibliographical references and index.
    Summary: Discusses the social position, culture, and wartime and peace-
time activities of the samurai warriors of ancient Japan.
    ISBN 1-56006-390-4 (lib. : alk. paper)
    1. Samurai—Social life and customs—Juvenile literature. [1. Samurai.
2. Japan—History—1185–1868.] I. Title. II. Series.
DS827.S3H46 1999
952'.02'088355—dc21
                                                98-30574
                                                  CIP
                                                       AC

Contents

Discovering the Humanity in Us All

Books in The Way People Live series focus on groups of people in a wide variety of circumstances, settings, and time periods. Some books focus on different cultural groups, others, on people in a particular historical time period, while others cover people involved in a specific event. Each book emphasizes the daily routines, personal and historical struggles, and achievements of people from all walks of life.

To really understand any culture, it is necessary to strip the mind of the common notions we hold about groups of people. These stereotypes are the archenemies of learning. It does not even matter whether the stereotypes are positive or negative; they are confining and tight. Removing them is a challenge that's not easily met, as anyone who has ever tried it will admit. Ideas that do not fit into the templates we create are unwelcome visitors—ones we would prefer remain quietly in a corner or forgotten room.

The cowboy of the Old West is a good example of such confining roles. The cowboy was courageous, yet soft-spoken. His time (it is always a he, in our template) was spent alternatively saving a rancher's daughter from certain death on a runaway stagecoach, or shooting it out with rustlers. At times, of course, he was likely to get a little crazy in town after a trail drive, but for the most part, he was the epitome of inner strength. It is disconcerting to find out that the cowboy is human, even a bit childish. Can it really be true that cowboys would line up to help the cook on the trail drive grind coffee, just hoping he would give them a little stick of peppermint candy that came with the coffee shipment? The idea of tough cowboys vying with one another to help "Coosie" (as they called their cooks) for a bit of candy seems silly and out of place.

So is the vision of Eskimos playing video games and watching MTV, living in prefab housing in the Arctic. It just does not fit with what "Eskimo" means. We are far more comfortable with snow igloos and whale blubber, harpoons and kayaks.

Although the cultures dealt with in Lucent's The Way People Live series are often historically and socially well known, the emphasis is on the personal aspects of life. Groups of people, while unquestionably affected by their politics and their governmental structures, are more than those institutions. How do people in a particular time and place educate their children? What do they eat? And how do they build their houses? What kinds of work do they do? What kinds of games do they enjoy? The answers to these questions bring these cultures to life. People's lives are revealed in the particulars and only by knowing the particulars can we understand these cultures' will to survive and their moments of weakness and greatness.

This is not to say that understanding politics does not help to understand a culture. There is no question that the Warsaw ghetto, for example, was a culture that was brought about by the politics and social ideas of Adolf

Hitler and the Third Reich. But the Jews who were crowded together in the ghetto cannot be understood by the Reich's politics. Their life was a day-to-day battle for existence, and the creativity and methods they used to prolong their lives is a vital story of human perseverance that would be denied by focusing only on the institutions of Hitler's Germany. Knowing that children as young as five or six outwitted Nazi guards on a daily basis, that Jewish policemen helped the Germans control the ghetto, that children attended secret schools in the ghetto and even earned diplomas—these are the things that reveal the fabric of life, that can inspire, intrigue, and amaze.

Books in The Way People Live series allow both the casual reader and the student to see humans as victims, heroes, and onlookers. And although humans act in ways that can fill us with feelings of sorrow and revulsion, it is important to remember that "hero," "predator," and "victim" are dangerous terms. Heaping undue pity or praise on people reduces them to objects, and strips them of their humanity.

Seeing the Jews of Warsaw only as victims is to deny their humanity. Seeing them only as they appear in surviving photos, staring at the camera with infinite sadness, is limiting, both to them and to those who want to understand them. To an object of pity, the only appropriate response becomes "Those poor creatures!" and that reduces both the quality of their struggle and the depth of their despair. No one is served by such two-dimensional views of people and their cultures.

With this in mind, The Way People Live series strives to flesh out the traditional, two-dimensional views of people in various cultures and historical circumstances. Using a wide variety of primary quotations—the words not only of the politicians and government leaders, but of the real people whose lives are being examined—each book in the series attempts to show an honest and complete picture of a culture removed from our own by time or space.

By examining cultures in this way, the reader will notice not only the glaring differences from his or her own culture, but also will be struck by the similarities. For indeed, people share common needs— warmth, good company, stability, and affirmation from others. Ultimately, seeing how people really live, or have lived, can only enrich our understanding of ourselves.

The Emergence of the Samurai

Although fighting men played a prominent role in Japanese history from the nation's beginning, the class of warriors known as samurai did not emerge until the twelfth century A.D. By that time, many small chiefdoms had been unified into a central state headed by an emperor or empress who was believed to be divine. The imperial court was located at Heian-kyo (now Kyoto), where the reigning monarch lived in a splendid palace, surrounded by men and women of noble birth.

Despite the prosperity of the court, unification of Japan was by no means complete. Rebellious warlords still challenged the authority of the emperor periodically, and fierce bands of Ainu (the original natives) still resisted subjugation. However, the good life of the imperial court was so far removed from such matters that emperors increasingly neglected to provide adequate protection for their subjects. In his study of early Japan, Jonathan Norton Leonard writes:

When landholders found they could no longer depend on royal officials for protection against outlaws or predatory neighbors, they armed their sons and retainers [servants] and put themselves under the leadership of chiefs renowned for fighting ability. . . . To gain additional strength for defense or offense, the warrior-chiefs of each small region banded together and offered their services to more important lords. In return for this support the lords

agreed to protect the minor chiefs and their followers and to share with them any booty that they might win. The lords in turn pledged allegiance to still loftier noblemen who were members of some ancient and mighty family, or at least claimed to be.[1]

This arrangement was similar to the feudal system of medieval Europe wherein lords protected vassals in return for their services. In medieval Japan, the relationship between warriors and clan chiefs was very intense. Mikiso Hane, author of a work on premodern Japan, says, "Once a master-vassal relationship was entered into, ideally the vassal was expected to dedicate his entire life to the service of his master. In return for his loyalty and services, the master was expected to reward him." Moreover, a kinship bond, either real or assumed, existed between vassal and overlord. "The lord-vassal relationship was viewed as a father-son relationship,"[2] observes Hane.

As a corollary to this feudal arrangement, a strict code of warrior behavior emerged, no doubt fostered by clan chiefs whose very existence depended upon a highly trained corps of dedicated fighting men. This code, later known as Bushido (way of the warrior), called upon a warrior to willingly sacrifice his life in the service of his master. Such an act was felt to be worthy of the highest honor and respect. It was during the twelfth century that warriors who lived and died by that code became known as samurai, meaning "those who serve."

Rule of the Shoguns

In the latter part of the twelfth century, two rival clans, the Taira and Minamoto, provided military assistance to the emperor. After putting down the emperor's enemies, the two clans turned against each other in bitter conflicts that continued for a quarter of a century. The Minamoto clan eventually defeated the Taira clan, and in 1192, the successful leader, Minamoto Yoritomo, had himself appointed shogun (military leader) by the emperor.

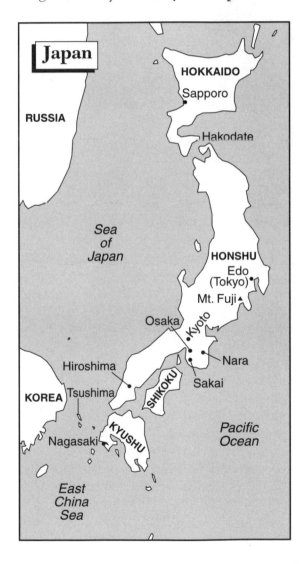

Traditionally, the title of shogun was a temporary position, but Yoritomo made it permanent after stripping the emperor of political authority. The real power was transferred to the *bakufu*, a centralized form of government created and headed by Yoritomo. (*Bakufu* is a military term meaning "tent government.") The new government established order after years of unrest brought about by interclan fighting.

After only seven years of rule, Yoritomo was killed in a fall from a horse, an event that threw *bakufu* officials into near panic. However, Yoritomo's widow, Masako, managed to hold the government together with the assistance of her family, the Hojo clan. For the next one hundred years, members of the Hojo clan ruled behind the scenes as regents, or advisers, to the hereditary shoguns.

Early in the fourteenth century, the Hojo regents were overthrown by the Ashikaga clan. Although the Ashikaga shoguns were cultured men who patronized the arts and built beautiful palaces and shrines, they were unable to prevent rival clans from attacking each other. Moreover, isolated in their luxurious palaces, they were completely removed from the economic and social problems of the growing nation.

Tokugawa Period

Consequently, throughout the fifteenth and sixteenth centuries Japan became a multitude of armed camps headed by powerful warlords, or daimyo, meaning "great name." Castle strongholds and military forts dotted the countryside. Clashes between rival clans as well as uprisings led by oppressed peasants became common. This *Sengoku*, or civil war period (1467–1576), was characterized by full-scale warfare with a complete lack of central authority to reestablish order.

Although the samurai were primarily soldiers, many excelled in arts and philosophy. In these pursuits, the samurai typically exhibited the same type of discipline that characterized their martial skills.

In the latter part of the sixteenth century, three strong leaders emerged in succession who subdued the warring daimyo and united the country. The last of these leaders, Tokugawa Ieyasu, became shogun in 1603. For the next two-and-a-half centuries, Tokugawa shoguns maintained peace with an iron hand. They also isolated Japan from the rest of the world. Foreigners were expelled and Japanese citizens were forbidden to leave.

In 1853 Commodore Matthew Perry of the U.S. Navy arrived in Tokyo Bay with warships. His official mission was to initiate a trading relationship between Japan and the United States, thereby breaking the long years of isolation. Unsure of how to deal with

Perry and the widespread anxiety caused by his arrival, the Tokugawa shogunate came under serious criticism by dissenters.

Under extreme pressure from the opposition movement, the last Tokugawa shogun resigned in 1868. Political power was restored to Emperor Meiji, or at least to those acting in his name. (He was only fifteen years old when he ascended the throne.) The Meiji Restoration, or enlightened rule, brought an end not only to the shogunate and the *bakufu* but to the samurai class as well. By 1876, all special class privileges that had been enjoyed by the samurai for centuries were abolished.

The Samurai Image

Obviously, these events were traumatic ones for the once-powerful samurai. Throughout the centuries dominated by shoguns, they had evolved from servants to military leaders and finally to military dictators. However, the samurai were never a homogeneous group. Within their ranks, a complex system of subclasses existed. At the top were wealthy chieftains, while at the opposite end of the scale impoverished samurai barely eked out a living. In between the two extremes were numerous social levels with differing lifestyles, privileges, and responsibilities.

Although the samurai warriors of Japan ceased to exist as a distinct group well over a century ago, their stories still capture the imag-

ination of the public through books, movies, plays, and art. Most portrayals of the samurai focus on their exploits in battle, their ferocity, their extraordinary swordsmanship, their mastery of the martial arts, and the strict code of discipline by which they lived and died.

While that picture is an accurate representation of samurai life at a particular time in their history, it is only one of many phases through which samurai culture passed during seven centuries of existence. It is less well known, for example, that the first samurai were mounted archers, more skilled with bows and arrows than with swords.

Even more surprising is that many samurai warriors became scholars, poets, artists, and philosophers who took pleasure in such delicate pastimes as the fine handwriting with ink and brush known as calligraphy, flower arranging, and the tea ceremony. Probably the most overlooked aspect of samurai life is the domestic roles they played in everyday life. Warriors were also sons, husbands, and fathers faced with economic and domestic responsibilities in their own households. Their families were samurai, too, and were expected to exhibit the same rigid discipline as the warriors themselves.

First and foremost, however, the samurai were warriors, a role that took precedence over all others. Their profession was fighting and their objective was to kill the enemies of their masters with total disregard for their own lives.

Professional Warriors

Long before the samurai appeared, Japanese warriors had been fighting almost continuously in battles against rival clans and against native peoples, and even attempted invasions of Korea. Thus, the samurai did not invent many of the combat techniques and military equipment with which they were associated, but when the samurai class emerged in the twelfth century, these warriors gradually put their own distinctive mark upon arms, armor, and the art of combat.

The Way of the Horse and Bow

Horses were used in Japanese warfare from very early times, as evidenced by statues and artifacts found in tombs of early chieftains.

The samurai class came into being during the civil wars that plagued Japan in the twelfth century. Although they would become almost exclusively identified with the sword (like that carried here by the samurai officer), samurai were known to be skilled in a variety of weapons such as the naginata *(carried here by common men-at-arms).*

The first samurai continued the tradition, becoming horsemen of great skill and daring. Because the principal weapon at this time was the bow and arrow, early samurai exploits were spoken of in Japanese war tales as the "Way of the Horse and Bow." This description referred not only to a way of fighting, but also to a code of behavior by which warriors lived.

Bows were made in a variety of lengths for various purposes, but war bows were seven to eight feet long and very difficult to pull. According to martial arts experts Oscar Ratti and Adele Westbrook, "These bows were made of several lengths of wood (usually selected qualities of bamboo) glued together with a characteristic bend at the end. . . . The bowstrings were made by skilled specialists from long fibers of hemp, sinews, or silk (silk being used generally for ceremonial bows)."[3] Warriors always carried extra bowstrings in their quivers or in special pouches.

A quiver of arrows was worn on a warrior's right side so he could quickly withdraw the arrows and fire them as he galloped along. Arrows were tipped with many different kinds of points, including signaling points that made whistling sounds as they moved through the air.

The quickness and force with which a skilled archer could shoot an arrow was remarkable. Stephen Turnbull, an authority on samurai warfare, tells of a duel between two warriors, Tametomo and Koreyuki, in which the latter fired an arrow at the former and missed. Before Koreyuki could slip another arrow into his bow, Tametomo shot back. Turnbull describes the event:

[The arrow] pierced the pommel of Koreyuki's saddle, and cutting through the skirt of his armor and his own body too, went through the cantle [rear part of a saddle] and stuck out three inches be-

This engraving shows an early samurai devoted to the "Way of the Horse and Bow." Arrows were fired in quick succession until the samurai could close with an enemy and attack with his sword.

yond. For a moment he seemed to be held in the saddle by the arrow, but suddenly he fell head first to the ground. The arrow remained in the saddle and the horse ran out to the river bed.[4]

Although they were not as important as the bow, swords of various sizes and types were also part of a samurai's arsenal in the early days. They were used mainly for close-quarter fighting. A great variety of spears were utilized also. One of these, the *naginata*, was a curved blade fixed to the end of a pole several feet long. The *naginata* was known as a woman's spear because samurai girls were taught to use it from an early age. A device called a *kumade* resembling a long-handled garden rake was used to grab the clothing or helmet of enemy horsemen and unseat them as they galloped by.

Samurai Armor

For defense, samurai archers depended upon body armor and the speed of their horses. Even though samurai horses were fast and had great endurance, they were not able to carry extremely heavy loads. Consequently, samurai armor was kept as lightweight as possible. It was made of dozens of small, scalelike pieces of overlapping metal. The metal pieces, called lamellae (la-MEL-ee), were lacquered, perforated, and laced together in intricate patterns with brilliantly colored cords.

Lightweight armor not only spared the horse, but had other advantages as well. Historian Jonathan Norton Leonard explains, "A samurai's armor only weighed about 25 pounds, allowing its wearer to leap with agility through rice paddies and over castle walls. In addition, it could be folded into a compact box for easy carrying when not in use, and if cut by a sword it could be mended by lacing on new lamellae."[5]

In dressing for battle, a high-ranking samurai first put on a simple one-piece undergarment followed by a short-sleeved kimono called an armor robe. He then pulled on a pair of baggy pantaloons and tucked the armor robe inside them. Both pantaloons and robes were made from brightly colored, richly patterned fabrics.

Next the warrior fastened around his legs a pair of shin guards made from padded cloth or leather and reinforced with metal inserts. On his feet, he wore sandals or shoes of various designs. A set of thigh guards made of lamellae protected the exposed thighs of a horseman while riding. Next came a pair of cloth sleeves

Common samurai armor made of lamellae pieces laced together with colorful cords. The lightweight armor allowed for greater freedom of movement and spared a samurai's horse the burden of a heavier load.

reinforced with leather or metal. These were quite cumbersome, and as a rule, archers wore them only on their left arms in order to keep their right arms free for shooting.

Lamellar body armor, held together by colorful silken cords, fitted snugly around the warrior's upper torso. Often, a breastplate of beautifully decorated leather covered the front. Several lamellar panels hung down from the waist to protect his lower torso. Broad flaps were attached at the shoulders for added protection there. All the components were tied together in the back with a special knot. When worn, this type of armor (called *yoroi*) had a very boxlike appearance.

A warrior's helmet was made of iron and was elaborately decorated to show his status and clan affiliation. Underneath the helmet, he wore a padded cap to ease the weight of the helmet, or his own hair was tied up in a bun and pulled through a hole in the top of the helmet.

To protect the back of his neck, a wide band made of lamellae was attached to the edge of the helmet. In addition, a metal neck protector and face mask were worn, giving the warrior an extremely fierce appearance. A fully dressed samurai of high rank was an intimidating sight. There was no mistaking who he was, the rank he held, or the seriousness of his purpose.

Archery Training

Firing volleys of arrows from a bow while charging the enemy either on foot or while galloping at full speed on a horse was no small accomplishment. In this excerpt from *Secrets of the Samurai: The Martial Arts of Feudal Japan*, Oscar Ratti and Adele Westbrook tell how archers were trained.

"The training program for archers was based upon repeated attempts to hit both fixed and mobile targets while on foot as well as on horseback. The major fixed targets were the large target, the deer target, and the round target. The first . . . was set thirty-three bowlengths and measured sixty-two inches in diameter. The second consisted of a deer's silhouette covered with deer skin and marked to indicate the vital spots to be hit; and the third consisted of a round board, stuffed and then covered with strong hide. There are indications that these targets were often hung from poles and set in motion in order to develop skill in hitting targets whose movement would render them more elusive and difficult to pierce from a distance.

Training on horseback, naturally, was obviously more aristocratic, in both nature and tradition, than training on foot. It demanded great coordination in controlling a galloping horse, while simultaneously releasing arrow after arrow against a series of different targets which might be either fixed or in motion."

Live dogs were also used as targets, but Buddhism put an end to this practice, as Ratti and Westbrook explain.

"Revulsion at the sight of this pointless slaughter, prompted and deepened by the spreading of Buddhism's civilizing influence throughout Japanese society, resulted in edicts which commanded that the archers use non-lethal arrows with large round arrowheads in these dog-shoots, while the dogs were to be outfitted with special, padded corselets."

Samurai were trained to fire arrows while either mounted or afoot. Since their enemies were often samurai also, samurai archers were drilled on hitting stationary and moving targets.

Under ordinary circumstances, the act of donning armor was a solemn ritual, with the wearer being assisted by lesser-ranking samurai. In times of heightened danger, however, a warrior's armor was always preassembled on a hanger or stand so he could slip into it quickly.

Not all samurai fought on horseback. Many were foot soldiers of lesser rank. Although their armor had all the basic pieces, it was much simpler than that of higher-ranking warriors, and far less protective. The main part of the armor, called *do-maru*, was a simple tunic of lamellae that wrapped around the warrior's body.

Combat Tactics

As ferocious as samurai warriors were, their battle tactics in the field were surprisingly formal. Opposing sides would face each other a few hundred yards apart. Each side would begin by firing volleys of arrows at each other from a distance. Then individual samurai would advance and shout out challenges to worthy opponents to meet them in private duels. Such a challenge, recorded in *The Tales of the Heike*, a collection of war stories compiled in the thirteenth century, reads:

> Then Ashikaga Matataro . . . stood up in the stirrups and shouted loudly: "I am Ashikaga Matataro Takatsuna, aged 17, son of Ashikaga no Taro Toshitsuna of Shimotsuke, descended in the tenth generation from Tawara Toda Hidesato . . . here I stand to meet any on the side of [the enemy] who dares to face me."[6]

Warrior after warrior would call out their challenges, and very soon many individual duels would be taking place. As fighting intensified, duels would merge into a general melee until one side had subdued the other. It was

The back view of samurai armor (left) shows the colorful cords that held the shoulder plates together and allowed the samurai more upper-arm mobility. The front of a samurai helmet (right) always carried some device that indicated the warrior's clan affiliation.

Splendidly Dressed Warriors

Samurai warlords were very concerned with appearance and lavished great care and expense upon their armor and weapons. The following descriptions of grandly attired samurai going into battle are taken from *Genji & Heike,* translated by Helen Craig McCullough.

"That day, Yoshitsune wore a red brocade tunic, a suit of armor with purple-shaded lacing, and a horned helmet. At his waist, he had fastened a sword with gilt bronze fittings; on his back, he carried a quiver containing arrows fledged with black-banded eagle feathers. An inch-wide strip of paper was wound leftwise around the left-hand grip of his rattan-wrapped bow, apparently as a sign that he was the commander in chief for the battle that day. . . .

That day, Lord Kiso wore a tunic of red brocade, a suit of armor laced with thick Chinese damask, and a horned helmet. At his side, he had strapped a magnificent long sword; high on his back, there was a quiver holding the few arrows that remained from his earlier battles, all fledged with the tails of eagle feathers. He grasped a bow wrapped with rattan and sat in a gold-edged saddle astride his famous horse Oniashige [Roan Demon], a very stout and brawny animal. Standing in the stirrups, he announced his name in a mighty shout. . . .

The commander-in-chief, Koremori, was twenty-three years old, more splendid in deportment than any painter's brush could depict. For the journey [military campaign], he wore a red brocade tunic and a suit of green-laced armor, and he rode a white-dappled reddish horse with a saddle edged in gold. The deputy commander, Tadanori, wore a blue tunic and a suit of armor with flame-red lacing, and he rode a stout and brawny black horse with a gold-flecked lacquer saddle. The army was a magnificent sight as it departed—the horses, the saddles, the armor, the helmets, the bows and arrows and swords—even the daggers seemed to gleam."

the custom for victors to cut off the heads of slain opponents, especially important ones, as proof of success. The severed heads would then be taken back to the camp and presented to the warlord on whose behalf the battle was fought.

Warriors on the losing side who were not killed in battle would almost always be executed, often in very ignominious and painful ways. Therefore, many defeated samurai chose to die by their own hand. By the thirteenth century, a distinct method of suicide had developed called seppuku, also known by its more vulgar name, hara-kiri, meaning "to cut the belly." Such an act purportedly freed the person's spirit before death.

Sometimes, seppuku was committed by many people at one time. In a study of samurai traditions, John Newman tells of such an event that took place in 1331 at the end of a fierce clan struggle. "On the last day [of the battle] the regent Takatoki set fire to his headquarters and withdrew to Toshoji temple, where he committed suicide with 800 of his followers."[7]

Samurai Women at War

Samurai women were rarely combat soldiers, but, as Leonard writes, "They were expected to exhibit the same loyalty and bravery as the men, and occasionally a woman exceptionally endowed with these qualities won an honored place in the warrior coterie."[8] Tomoe Gozen, the wife of a powerful Minamoto warlord, was such a person whose remarkable fighting talents have been immortalized in samurai folklore.

In last-ditch battles, women and children often fought beside their fathers, sons, and husbands, or took matters into their own hands to save honor. An example of the latter is Lady Nii, a high-ranking member of the Taira clan. She was also grandmother to Emperor Antoku, who was only seven years old in 1185 when the Minamoto clan won a great victory that drove the Taira clan out of power.

As the Minamoto forces approached the capital, high-ranking members of the Taira clan fled, taking the young emperor with them. They boarded a naval vessel but were defeated soon afterward in a fierce sea battle. Knowing there would be no mercy for the young emperor, Lady Nii took action, described in *The Tale of the Heike*. "She draped her two gray inner robes over her head, hitched up her divided skirt of glossed silk, tucked the Bead Strand under her arm and the Sword into her belt [symbols of imperial

Lady Warriors

Not only did samurai women stand by their men in times of crisis, but a few of them were warriors themselves according to Japanese chronicles from the early feudal period. In *Women Warriors*, author David E. Jones describes the exploits of intrepid samurai women.

"The beloved Japanese war epic, *Heike Monagatari*, features many women warriors. . . . Tomoe Gozen was the most famous woman warrior of medieval Japan. In one battle, after she had killed several enemies in single combat, the leader of the attacking force, Uchida Iyeyoshi, attempted to capture Tomoe himself. During the skirmish, with swords flashing, her sleeve was torn off as her attacker sought to drag her from her horse. Infuriated, she wheeled her charger and severed Uchida's head, a trophy she later presented to her husband. . . . Shizuka Gozen, mistress of the national hero Yoshitsune, accompanied her lover in many battles in the late twelfth century and was conspicuous in the defense of Horikawa Castle in 1185. . . .

Koman was a twelfth-century Japanese woman warrior involved in many daring exploits. At a battle between the Taira and Minamoto on Lake Biwa, Koman saved the Minamoto banner from capture by swimming to shore with it in her teeth while Taira arrows rained around her. . . .

When the great Shogun Yoritomo died, his wife Hojo Masa-Ko took control of the government. Born the daughter of a samurai family in 1157, she functioned well in a world of military men and maintained the loyalty of the army. . . .

In April of 1201, members of the Taira clan fought for their lives defending Echigo Castle against overwhelming forces. Hangaku, a samurai's daughter and an excellent archer, dressed in soldier's attire, stood on the highest tower of the castle and launched her arrows into the enemy host with telling effect. Desperate to negate her firepower, they shot her in the back, a very unsamurai act."

power], and took the Emperor in her arms and said, 'I'm only a woman, but I don't intend to fall into enemy hands. I go where His Majesty goes. Follow me, you whose hearts are loyal to him!' She walked to the side of the ship."[9] Assuring the frightened child that a place of pure bliss awaited him, she jumped with him into the sea.

Women were also responsible for some of the more grim duties associated with samurai war. One of these was preparing the severed heads of enemies for display. Turnbull describes this grisly procedure: "The heads would be washed, the hair combed, and the resulting trophy made presentable by cosmetics—all tasks performed with great delicacy by the women of the daimyo's court. The heads would then be mounted on a spiked wooden board, with labels for identification . . . one by one the heads would be brought before him [the daimyo] for comment."[10]

Changes in Weaponry and Armor

As political circumstances changed throughout the centuries, so did weapons and armor. One of these changes was the gradual shift from bows and arrows to spears and swords as the principal weapons. Changes in armor naturally followed. Mounted archers wearing heavy armor were very effective in wide open places, but as martial arts teacher Fred Neff explains,

As time went by, the samurai often had to fight on rough, wooded, and mountainous terrain, where it was difficult to remain on horseback. The bow and arrow was slowly abandoned, along with heavy armor. Light, flexible armor that gave more freedom of movement when fighting with

Samurai armor was created by skilled craftsmen who often gave their work an artistic flair. Especially during the peaceful Tokugawa period, armor, such as this dolphin helmet, looked more like pieces of art.

swords was developed. Later, in peaceful times, armor further evolved into very ornate dress uniforms now recognized as works of art.[11]

As swords and spears grew in popularity, disputes arose among warriors about which was more effective in combat. Unlike swords, whose purpose was to slash or pierce the enemy (if the warrior could get close enough), heavy spears were better for knocking armored warriors from their horses. In terms of aesthetic value, however, swords were prized. Over time, samurai swords took on a mystical quality and were considered to be the very essence, or soul, of a samurai's being.

During the peaceful Tokugawa era, only samurai were allowed to wear two swords, a long, curved blade called a *katana* and a shorter one known as a *wakizashi*. Samurai swords were extremely sharp. A *katana* could literally

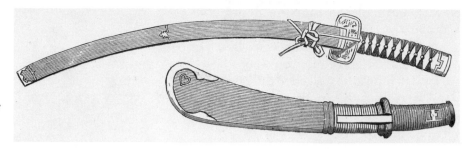

The long katana *and the shorter* wakizashi *became the symbol of the samurai. Like the samurai's armor, his swords were well made and ornate.*

cut a person in half when wielded by a warrior trained in the art of swordsmanship. Fine swords were not only effective weapons, but works of art as well, with beautifully decorated handles and scabbards. Before being used in battle, new swords were often tested on the bodies of executed criminals. Sometimes new swords were used to carry out the execution itself.

Japanese swordsmiths were among the best in the world, having solved the problem of making blades pliable enough not to break when struck against an enemy's armor yet still hard enough to hold a razor-sharp edge through repeated usage. Leonard describes the process:

> For the core, or interior, of such a blade, they used comparatively soft, laminated metal that would resist breaking. The blade's exterior and edge, however, were made of different grades of hard steel welded together into a sandwich that was folded and hammered out as many as 20 times, giving it more than a million laminations. This outer "skin" of steel could be made even harder by heating and sudden cooling. . . . The final result was a sword blade of soft, nonbrittle metal enclosed in a thin layer of hard steel.[12]

A great deal of ceremony went into the making of a blade, and swordsmiths were highly respected for their skill. As beautiful as

the swords were, however, their purpose was a deadly one. As Turnbull expresses it, "The semimystical Japanese sword was first and foremost a weapon for killing other samurai."[13]

Turnbull also believes that not all Japanese swords were exceptional, noting that Japan exported swords to China by the thousands in the fourteenth century. "The long ritual-like process by which a fine sword was forged has been often described. But here is the clearest evidence that such efforts must have been reserved for a minimum of special orders, and that the overwhelming number of swords must have been manufactured on a production line."[14]

In the sixteenth century, a matchlock gun called a harquebus was brought into Japan by Portuguese sailors. At first, warlords refused to adopt it. "It was somehow regarded as unsporting," Newman comments, "or perhaps they were like chess players who did not want an additional new piece on the board. In any case they did not use them."[15] They were first used on a large scale in the late sixteenth century by Oda Nobunaga in his drive to unify the country.

Changes in Combat Tactics

Formal combat tactics were more likely to occur between rival clans in the more settled regions of Japan than in the rugged frontier areas, where samurai often fought guerrilla-like skirmishes against hostile natives. As it happened, the Taira clan was strong in the settled regions, being closely connected to the imperial court through intermarriage. On the other hand, their bitter rivals, the Minamoto, were strongest in the frontier regions and less sophisticated in courtly ways. A battle that occurred between the two clans in 1183 provides a good example of the decline of formal battle tactics.

Kiso Yoshinaka, a Minamoto warlord, made devastating raids upon Taira provinces from his mountain realm. In retaliation, the Taira sent an expedition against him in 1183. When the two armies met at the Pass of Kurikara high in the mountains, Yoshinaka promptly engaged the Taira in a traditional samurai battle. Being skilled at this type of fighting, the courtly Taira entered into the fray with great enthusiasm.

What they did not know, however, was that Yoshinaka was only stalling them until another contingent of his troops could block off their retreat. The real battle, a very untraditional one, was yet to come. Turnbull describes it:

As the sun set, Yoshinaka's encircling force arrived at the rear. . . . As the Taira reacted to this surprise, they met a further shock in the front. . . . [Yoshinaka's] men had rounded up a herd of oxen and tied

A troop of samurai marches with firearms. Although guns had been introduced to Japan in the sixteenth century, most samurai refused to use them, probably because they were cumbersome, had a slow rate of fire, and were prone to failure.

torches to their horns. The torches were fired and the enraged oxen whipped off along the pass . . . meanwhile, the [Minamoto] soldiers on the northern slope, who had been such gentlemen until then, charged forward in a screaming rush. There was nowhere to go except down into the valley of Kurikara, which [the Taira soldiers] thought had a safe exit. But the paths petered out, and Yoshinaka's detached forces were waiting for them in the dark.[16]

Further changes in traditional combat tactics were thrust upon the samurai as a result of the Mongol invasions of the thirteenth century. Twice in that century, Kublai Khan, the powerful ruler of China, sent vast armadas of ships and men to invade Japan. Facing serious external threats, samurai clans cooperated in defense of their lands. However, they found themselves at a great disadvantage. As H. Paul Varley explains in a study of Japanese history, "Unlike the Samurai of Japan, who were accustomed to single, man-to-man combat, the Mongols fought in organized units and used weapons such as catapults and exploding balls that were unfamiliar to the Japanese."[17]

With a big assist from the forces of nature, the Mongols were repelled. In both invasions, devastating storms sank the ships of the Mongols and left them stranded on the beaches

This woodcut shows a samurai general defeating an invading force of Mongol warriors. Because they were individually powerless against the hordes of Mongols, Japan's divided warlords united their forces against this foreign threat.

The Mongol forces of Kublai Khan (pictured) were twice repelled in their attempt to invade Japan.

to be killed by Japanese defenders. With the threat of invasion gone, samurai clans renewed their conflicts against one another.

During the latter part of the fifteenth century, neither the ruling shogun nor the imperial court was able to control competing daimyo. The result was constant civil strife. Moreover, the size of armies had greatly increased, augmented by hundreds of foot soldiers called *ashigaru,* or "light feet." This new style of warfare called for disciplined troop movements and imaginative strategy, both on the battlefield and in attacking or defending castle strongholds that dotted the countryside.

Civil strife was finally brought to an end in the late sixteenth century by three strong leaders, Oda Nobunaga, Toyotomi Hideyoshi, and Tokugawa Ieyasu. Within a few years, these able leaders unified the country and established peace. Knowing ambitious daimyo were the greatest threat to peace (they had all been daimyo themselves), Ieyasu put them and their samurai under rigid control. Life among the proud samurai changed drastically, but the strict discipline and training that had turned them into fighting men sustained them in peacetime as well.

Becoming a Samurai Warrior

In spite of drastic changes through which samurai life passed, one thing remained constant—the rigid discipline and training it took to become a samurai. Whether the end result was a warrior, a bureaucrat, or an artist, a samurai was expected to excel. This does not mean all samurai lived up to expectations, of course, but the tradition of dedication to one's calling was always present.

Where and by what means a samurai warrior was educated and trained depended upon the time period in question, since educational opportunities increased through time. During all times, however, the extent and quality depended upon family status, and a great gulf separated high and low ranks. Sons of elite samurai attended special institutes or temples and had tutors to educate them in classical studies and the martial arts.

If sons in lower-class families attended school at all, they went to village schools or monasteries for basic learning, and were taught samurai skills at home by fathers and other male relatives. Sometimes they were apprenticed to sword or archery masters. In later periods, clans themselves sometimes set up schools for low-rank samurai boys. In all time periods and social ranks, learning the martial arts was paramount. Samurai boys were first given warrior clothing and wooden swords at the age of five or six.

Formal education for samurai girls was considered of less importance, but upper-class girls had more opportunities than those of lower rank. Both received instruction in reading and writing whenever possible, but at every social level, training at home in the roles of wives, mothers, and household managers was of highest priority. In addition, girls and women were expected to defend themselves and to exhibit the same stoic attitude toward life and death as the male members of the family. To this end they were given lessons in the use of weapons, particularly the dagger and *naginata.*

Self-Control

Although it was vital for a warrior to be proficient with weapons, being skillful with a bow or sword meant far more than learning how to shoot arrows or swing a blade. A successful samurai had to condition not only his body, but his mind and spirit as well. In combat, those elements worked together, and all were essential to success. "Many years of hard training and suffering were needed to develop the balance, timing, and self-control required to use the sword properly," martial arts teacher Fred Neff explains. "Mental preparation was also a major ingredient of the training. A battle involved not only physical skills, but the ability to control emotions."[18]

A samurai's training, therefore, began early, before other habits or social patterns could be established. To help them learn to endure pain and suffering, young samurai boys were subjected to grueling physical hardships such as fasting, marching barefoot in the snow, and maintaining rigid postures for long intervals. Moreover, all this had to be borne without complaining or showing signs of discomfort. In such challenging lessons as these, samurai were often aided by spiritual beliefs.

Spirituality and Samurai Training

The earliest spiritual beliefs in Japan were called Shinto, a religious system that is still prominent today. Until the twentieth century, emperors and empresses were believed to be direct descendants of Shinto gods. Another religious system, Buddhism, was introduced from China in the fifth century A.D. There was resistance at first, but the two systems eventually learned to coexist peacefully. Although Shinto was influential on samurai life (an important deity was the Shinto war god, Hachiman), it was Buddhism that had the most profound effect.

Buddhism was initiated in India in the sixth century B.C. by a wealthy young prince named Gautama. According to stories about him, he renounced his life of luxury in order to seek spiritual enlightenment. During his quest, he came to believe that suffering is an inescapable part of human life but humans may rise above it by giving up worldly desires and living unselfish lives. Before reaching that blissful state, however, a person may have to be reborn into the world and suffer through many lifetimes. Eventually a devout seeker

---

Proper Education for a Samurai

Just how much education a warrior needed beyond mastery of fighting skills was a matter of some disagreement among samurai themselves, as this excerpt from *Zen and the Way of the Sword* by Winston L. King indicates.

"Just how far this literary culture could extend beyond the basics was a matter of differing emphases. The elements most often included in the proper samurai education were poem writing . . . and the tea ceremony . . . because of its austere dignity and simplicity. . . .

There were, as might be expected, some stalwart, unreconstructed leaders who hewed close to the ancient warrior-caste gospel of the Samurai Way as one of a purely sword and spear culture. . . . Samurai-lord Kato Kiyomosa (1562–1611), was one such. . . . He perceived the warrior-born to have but one duty: to firmly grasp his swords and die. The cultured arts of poetry making and reading were bound to have a womanizing influence, in his opinion, and anyone who practiced dancing should be ordered to commit suicide.

But others, even his contemporaries, disagree with him. They believed that the warrior (bushi) should be true to the ancient meaning of his name: the bushi as a man of both the sword and letters who never let the letters get out of hand. Of course, the nonmartial arts could never be a true samurai's greatest concern, and learning for learning's sake was not for the samurai. But the warrior need not thereby be an uncultured boor. . . . Especially valuable was learning that was practical and functional, a kind of farsighted wisdom, a basic knowledge of the Chinese philosophical-ethical classics, and on the *very* practical level the ability to write a good hand."

achieves a state of serenity called nirvana in which pain and anguish are overcome.

As Buddhism spread throughout Asia, it took on many different forms. Pure Land Buddhism taught that paradise could be reached by all true seekers simply by repeating the name of the Buddha over and over. This branch of Buddhism appealed to samurai and others who could not spend their entire lives seeking enlightenment. Of course, to attain paradise, believers also had to live simple lives of denial and self-control. Since many samurai were already doing that, Pure Land Buddhism gave their lives spiritual support.

During the thirteenth century, a branch of Buddhism called Zen, introduced from China, had an even greater appeal for samurai. Zen required students to meditate, maintain strict body postures, and to ponder illogical questions to rid the mind of traditional ways of thinking. Through steadfast practice of Zen techniques, sudden enlightenment might be attained. Neither long-term study nor an endless cycle of deaths and re-

births was necessary. Even meditation could be done in the course of daily activities.

"This type of Buddhism encouraged individual study and growth," Neff states. "People who embraced a Zen way of life were expected to undergo very tough physical, mental, emotional, and spiritual training. Zen played a large part in developing the samurai's ability to undergo extremes of hardship and pain without complaint."[19] Moreover, Zen was open to anyone who could endure the rigorous training, women included. There were Zen nunneries where women practiced and taught Zen, many of them from the samurai class.

Zen also taught adherents to face death without fear or loss of dignity. A story is told about a Zen master who was confronted by a hostile rebel general. When the general commanded the Zen master to bow down to him, the Zen master refused. Historian John Newman reports what happened next: "The general shouted, 'Don't you know you are looking at a man who can run you through without blink-

The Great Buddha at Kamakura was erected under the patronage of Minamoto Yoritomo. Zen Buddhism appealed to the samurai because it preached that enlightenment could come through the practice of Buddhist techniques rather than time-consuming study. Samurai were adept at practicing skills but could not afford the demands of constant study.

A suit of samurai armor bearing Buddhist inscriptions on the breastplate. Buddhism aligned well with the samurai ethic because it emphasized self-control and rigorous mental and physical training.

ing?' The Zen master replied in a strong voice, 'And you are looking at a man who can be run through without blinking.' The general stared at him, made a bow, and went away."[20] Other stories tell of Zen followers who were not as lucky as this one, but who remained unflinching even when violent death overtook them.

Mental Alertness

Another facet of samurai training requiring both mental and physical qualities was preparedness. A samurai's mind had to be alert and his body ready to react at any time or place. In her study of samurai life, Catharina Blomberg notes that famous sword masters "urged a severe mental discipline which entailed a constant alertness which bordered on the attainment of a sixth sense."[21] This sixth sense, a kind of intuition or insight, was not something that just happened. It had to be painfully acquired, as historian Jonathan Norton Leonard illustrates:

> A Japanese story tells of a young swordsman who apprenticed himself to a famous fencing master. One day, while cooking rice, he was given a painful whack with a wooden sword by his master. This treatment was repeated at unexpected hours of the day and night, until the youth learned never to relax his guard and became the greatest swordsman in the land.[22]

Lessons learned in youth carried over into adult life in direct ways. Stories are told of samurai escaping from sudden attacks by being able to sense the danger beforehand and repel it quickly. In one story, a samurai was doing calligraphy when he was suddenly attacked by a swordsman. Acting almost instinctively, the calligrapher flicked ink into the eyes of his attacker and escaped.

Another story tells of a Zen nun who was threatened by a sword-wielding man attracted by her beauty. She quickly rolled up a piece of paper and used it as a sword to attack his eyes. He was so astonished and amazed at her courage that he could not swing his sword. The nun then gave a mighty Zen shout that stunned him and caused him to fall down. (The Zen shout was taught to warriors in order to startle and terrorize their enemies.) As soon as the swordsman recovered his wits, he got up and ran.

Whether these stories were true or not, they served the purpose of impressing samurai

Zen masters taught the importance of completely focusing on whatever one was doing as well as remaining alert for, and unperturbed by, unexpected events. As John Newman notes in this story from *Bushido: The Way of the Warrior,* the fortitude of Zen adherents was sometimes tested by their friends as well as their enemies.

"After the importation of firearms at the end of the sixteenth century, a Chinese master happened to be visiting Japan where he was the honored guest of one of the local lords who, however, decided to test his realization [Zen skills]. The lord arranged that the master's tea bowl should be filled right to the brim at a meal. Although the master noticed this, he said nothing and lifted the bowl steadily to his lips. As he was about to drink, the lord gave a concealed signal and a gun was discharged in the next room. The master's hand did not shake and he quietly drank his tea without spilling a drop. The local lord was impressed and said, 'Weren't you a bit surprised when that gun went off?' The Zen master replied, 'Guns are the province of warriors, like you. That is nothing to do with a Zen priest like me.' The lord bowed his head in acquiescence and admiration, and they went on with the meal. Then, when the lord was about to sip tea from his cup, the master suddenly let out a tremendous Zen shout. The lord was very startled and the tea spilt. He turned to the master and said, 'Why did you do that? Look, the tea's all over my clothes.' To which the master answered, 'Why were you startled like that? The Zen shout has nothing to do with warriors like you, it's the business of Zen priests like me. Why did you react to my shout?'"

pupils with the need for readiness. Even at leisure activities, when playing a musical instrument, perhaps, or while performing dances, samurai had to be constantly on guard, for it was at such times that they were most vulnerable to surprise attacks.

Training for Mounted Archery

While young samurai were developing proper mental attitudes, they were also being instructed in the use of whatever weapons were in vogue at the time. Even in early days when the bow was the principal weapon, attitude and skill were inseparable, like two sides of the same coin. For example, in archery, the crucial moment is when the arrow is released from the bow. The more the archer thinks about this action, the less likely he is to hit the target. Consequently, archers were taught the importance of freeing thought from action.

This concept is expressed by Yagyu Munenori, a high-ranking samurai general and government official who wrote a treatise on the art of war in 1632: "Suppose you are shooting with a bow and you think you are shooting while you are shooting; then the aim of your bow will be inconsistent and unsteady. . . . When you shoot, unless you get rid of the idea of shooting, it is a sickness of archery."[23]

Breathing properly was also an important part of an archer's training. The proper time to release an arrow was just after inhaling, when the body is full of breath. The goal of such training was to learn a skill so thoroughly and to practice it so diligently that it could be done without conscious thought.

Riding skills were also a fundamental part of an archer's training, especially in the early days. Special training areas were set up where samurai shot arrows at targets as they galloped by on self-guiding horses. Winston L. King says in *Zen and the Way of the Sword*, "The mounted warrior and his horse were finely tuned to each other and worked together as one organism." As combat tactics changed, fewer samurai rode horses, but "even then," King continues, "the samurai ideal par excellence was that horsemanship should continue to be part of every young samurai's training."[24]

Training in Swordsmanship

As swords gained in prominence, many schools devoted to swordsmanship were established, each teaching the founder's particular techniques of fighting. In all schools, however,

Only dismounted archers, such as this one, were afforded the luxury of careful aim. The mounted samurai was trained not to concern himself with concentrated aim; his shooting had to become nearly instinctual through practice.

coordination of mind, body, and spirit (often based upon Buddhist principles) was emphasized.

The popularity of Buddhism among the samurai is somewhat paradoxical in that Buddhism advocates nonviolence. However, many sword masters had ways of rationalizing this fact. Yagyu Munenori, for instance, made a distinction between the "killing sword" and the "life-giving sword." He writes, "It may happen that myriad people suffer because of the evil of one man. In such a case, myriad people are saved by killing one man. Would this not be a true example of 'the sword that kills is the sword that gives life?'"[25]

Whether pupils were wielding killing swords or life-giving ones, Munenori instructed them in much the same manner as archers were instructed—to absorb and practice the techniques so thoroughly that wielding a sword became second nature. Munenori writes, "When what you have studied leaves your mind entirely, and practice also disappears, then, when you perform whatever art you are engaged in, you accomplish the techniques easily without being inhibited by concern over what you have learned, and yet without deviating from what you have learned."[26]

On the physical side, Munenori instructed his pupils in proper sword-fighting techniques such as how to force an adversary to make the first move, how to stay out of range of an enemy sword, how to fight with your back against the wall or in closed places, and how to defend yourself against multiple adversaries. Repeatedly, Munenori states that fighting techniques cannot be adequately explained in writing but must be learned from a teacher and practiced over and over.

One of the most renowned of all Japanese sword masters was Miyamoto Musashi. Munenori and Musashi were contemporaries, although in widely differing levels of samurai society. While Munenori was of the elite samurai class, Musashi was a *ronin*, or masterless samurai. Musashi set forth his instructions for sword fighting in 1643 in a work called *The Book of Five Rings*.

The word *rings* in the title refers to spheres or aspects of combat into which Musashi divided his work (which was originally handwritten on scrolls). In one section called the "Water Scroll," Musashi describes detailed sword-fighting techniques along with advice on how to maintain the proper mental state while fighting. His advice, gained from a long life of successful dueling, covers such

This early eighteenth-century painting depicts a sword-wielding samurai astride his horse. Samurai continually honed their sword-fighting skills, and they were expected never to be caught without their weapon at hand.

A Famous Swordsman

One of the greatest swordsmen in samurai history was Miyamoto Musashi. Although there are many legends about him, the few facts known about his life come from his own pen. When he was sixty years old, he wrote down the principles of his "school" of sword fighting in *The Book of Five Rings*. This excerpt is from a translation of that work by Thomas Cleary.

"The science of martial arts called the Individual School of Two Skies is something that I have spent many years refining. Now, wishing to reveal it in a book for the first time, I have ascended Mt. Iwato in the Higo province of Kyushu. Bowing to Heaven, paying respects to Kannon [Buddhist deity], I face the Buddha. I am Shinmen Musashi no Kami, Fujiwara no Genshin, a warrior born in the province of Harima, now sixty years old.

I have set my mind on the science of martial arts since my youth long ago. I was thirteen years old when I had my first duel. On that occasion I won over my opponent.

. . . At sixteen years of age I beat a powerful martial artist. . . . When I was twenty-one, I went to the capital city and met martial artists from all over the country. Although I engaged in numerous duels, never did I fail to attain victory.

After that, I traveled from province to province, meeting martial artists of the various schools. Although I dueled more than sixty times, never once did I lose. That all took place between the time I was thirteen years old and the time I was twenty-nine. . . . I subsequently practiced day and night in order to attain an even deeper principle, and spontaneously came upon the science of martial arts. I was about fifty years old at that time. . . .

Now, in composing this book, I have not borrowed the old sayings of Buddhism or Confucianism, nor do I make use of old stories from military records or books on military science. With Heaven and Kannon for mirrors, I take up the brush and begin to write, at 4:00 A.M. on the night of the tenth day of the tenth month, 1643."

matters as footwork, offensive and defensive sword strokes, and rhythm of movement. In the "Fire Scroll," Musashi discusses battle strategies ranging from duels between two swordsmen to battles between entire armies.

Both Munenori and Musashi also taught "no-sword" fighting techniques for those occasions when a samurai might be caught without a sword (which should never happen), or when his sword got broken in a fight or was forced from his hand. No-sword tactics taught samurai how to defend themselves by turning an adversary's strength and momentum against him, or how to use other objects such as metal fans or wooden staffs in an emergency.

Samurai Training and the Literary Arts

As mercenary soldiers, the first samurai came from outlying segments of Japanese society where action, strength, and proficiency with weapons was prized above all else. Many samurai from rural areas were farmers when not on military assignment. Others lived and fought native resistance groups on the wild frontier. Samurai such as these were judged by urban residents and imperial court members as uncouth barbarians.

However, as the court relied more and more upon powerful clans for support, samurai

Although samurai were foremost soldiers, they also pursued the arts and engaged in politics. Thus, many samurai learned to develop not only fighting skills but also social and cultural talents.

served as palace guards or performed other official duties, exposing them to a refined lifestyle. Some samurai became attached to the imperial court through politics and intermarriage (such as the Taira clan). Outside imperial circles, where clans joined together for protection, samurai began to be drawn from more sophisticated segments of society and often helped administer the vast estates of their clans. For these jobs, more than fighting skills were necessary. Summing up these changes, Martin Collcutt, Marius Jansen, and Isao Kumakura, authors of *Cultural Atlas of Japan*, write:

> As *bushi* [samurai] gained political power, they began to set the tone for the society

and culture. On the one hand, *bushi* were practitioners of the martial arts (*bu*) of "the way of the bow and arrow." On the other hand, they had to master skills of government and local administration which involved some measure of literacy and learning. . . . By the end of the 13th century the ideal of the warrior as one who should have mastered literary and administrative skills (*bun*) as well as the arts of war (*bu*) was already established.[27]

Even during some of the most violent periods in samurai history, literary skills and fine arts continued to flourish, supported by samurai in high places, often the shogun himself. "Many warriors were literate," Collcutt,

Jansen, and Kumakura observe. "Some, including Minamoto Yoritomo and his son Sanetomo and several of the Hojo regents [Yoritomo's successors] wrote poetry that was considered sufficiently accomplished to be included in major anthologies. Many other warriors participated in literary salons with nobles and monks and patronized painters, dramatists and craftsmen."[28]

Thus, from early times onward, education in fine arts, crafts, drama, and literature became a samurai ideal. Even the rough-hewn sword master Musashi (who reportedly never combed his hair or took a bath) admonished his pupils to gain knowledge other than fighting. "As human beings," he wrote, "it is essential for each of us to cultivate and polish our individual path."[29]

Many samurai were literate and professed great interest in literature and the arts. Some became art patrons while others painted or wrote poetry.

Teachers were mainly monks and courtiers. Oftentimes samurai whose masters had been killed or deposed supported themselves by teaching. The sources of knowledge were varied, but included Buddhist teachings, Chinese philosophy (such as the sayings of Confucius), and literary works of Japanese historians, philosophers, writers, and poets. Artisans taught such popular skills as calligraphy, painting, flower arranging, and poetry writing.

Not all samurai were literate, of course. Lower-class samurai in rural areas did not have time to study as well as fight, farm, and take care of their households, but as a rule, most samurai took advantage of cultural learning whenever they could.

Training for Peacetime

Samurai life and the training necessary for it underwent enormous changes during the Tokugawa period (1603–1853) when the country was unified and peace was enforced by powerful leaders. Two of the three great generals who accomplished unification were men from humble samurai backgrounds who had risen through the ranks. Knowing rebellious daimyo (like themselves) were the greatest threat to continued peace, steps were taken to neutralize them socially and economically.

"Weakening the daimyo economically proved easy," write Peter Spry-Leverton and Peter Kornicki in their study of Japanese history. "They were required, for example, to keep up a flow of presents to the shogun's household, and a close watch was kept to make sure they were spending suitably large sums on the presents."[30]

Another economic burden to keep the daimyo from becoming too powerful was a strict residence requirement. Daimyo and their families had to live in Edo (now Tokyo),

A painting of a daimyo on his way to the capital. One way the emperor tried to maintain peace during the Tokugawa period was to require all daimyo to live in the capital and to mandate when and for how long daimyo could return to their native provinces.

the capital city, and only the men were allowed to visit their estates periodically. While they were away, their families remained in Edo, virtually as hostages. Those daimyo who had not supported the Tokugawa regime were assigned fiefs (estates) in the far reaches of the country, which made traveling back and forth very expensive.

In social matters, daimyo had to get the shogun's permission for family marriages in order to forestall any troublesome alliances with other clans. Leonard explains the new situation in which the samurai found themselves:

The proud samurai were no longer country gentlemen living on their own estates

and ready to spring to arms at their lord's command. The higher ranks were bureaucrats or the equivalent of army officers. The lower ranks were soldiers. Almost all of them lived on salaries paid by the daimyo. Their weapons were provided for them and their movements and activities were closely restricted.[31]

Samurai were allowed to keep their swords, however. In fact, they were the only segment of the population allowed to be armed, as swords were confiscated from all other classes. But in the absence of war, the opportunity to use them diminished greatly. What to do with great numbers of unemployed

The Sword: Soul of a Samurai

After describing fighting techniques and weapons used by the samurai in *Zen and the Way of the Sword: Arming the Samurai Psyche,* author Winston L. King concludes the following about the importance of the sword.

"But of course, in Japan, swordsmanship outranked any and all other martial skills in prestige and importance. . . . Whatever other weapons the warrior might use—horse and armor, bow and arrow, halbert or spear, and even musket in later times—the sword, long or short, or long *and* short, was also worn as a kind of personal statement of the bearer's warrior spirit and status, of his pride as a man set above other classes of men. (Even samurai women wore their dirks, prepared to defend themselves and their honor.) Thus in the end, over and above all other weapons, the sword was, and has remained, the supreme symbol of the Japanese martial spirit and of a man's (and the nation's) vigor and pride. It was the aristocratic weapon of hundreds of years of internal warfare, the badge of warrior quality and supremacy in the age of the samurai when he was defined as the sword bearer, and one of the Three Sacred Treasures of the Imperial Throne.

Many students of swords and swordsmanship believe that the Japanese sword was the best ever made in terms of the quality of the steel in its blade and the sophistication and intensive care given to its making. Thus it represents not only the spiritual essence of the warrior class and national spirit, so to speak, but also the meticulous attention that Japanese have traditionally given to both craftsmanship and artistry."

This bronze sculpture depicts a warrior drawing his sword, a symbol of his manhood and his status as a samurai.

samurai became one of the major problems of the Tokugawa period. Obviously, the type of training and education samurai received had to change to suit a new style of life. Spry-Leverton and Kornicki write:

> The solution was to make them into a kind of governing class, to translate them from warriors to bureaucrats. This did not happen immediately, of course, for Ieyasu and his successors were not so confident of their powers to presume that military strength could be completely dispensed with. Nevertheless, in the course of the seventeenth century the education of sam-urai for a different role in society came to be seen as increasingly important and the curricula at the samurai schools combined the skills of the soldier with literary skills in the field of Chinese philosophy.[32]

Nevertheless, as in other times of adversity, samurai managed to adapt to changing conditions, for it was during the Tokugawa period that the famous code of Bushido was first written down. This work drew upon the principles of life, war, and honor by which centuries of samurai had lived. The code's appearance in written form was a highlight in samurai history.

The Code of Bushido

Before Japanese fighting men were known as samurai, they were called *bushi*, meaning "warrior." By adding the Japanese word *do*, which means "the way," *bushido* literally translates as "the way of the warrior." It refers to a set of principles by which samurai warriors guided their lives.

Samurai adhered to a code of duty and honor. Called Bushido, this warrior ethic was not codified throughout Japan early in the samurai era. Instead, different masters handed down their own versions of Bushido to their pupils.

Although samurai principles are usually referred to as a code of behavior, it is a mistake to think of Bushido as a precise set of rules and regulations. For centuries, ideals of honor, duty, and responsibility were not even written down. The first books about Bushido did not appear until the late seventeenth century, after the country was unified and civil wars had ceased. Writing about the code of Bushido, historian Winston L. King says:

> It is too strong a term to call the samurai ethos a "code.". . . It was not uniform, nor was it ever formally adopted by any group; samurai behavior varied from clan to clan and from period to period. It was at best a general operational social mode of behavior and attitudes, with some main themes and values persisting in one form or another throughout.[33]

The samurai themes and values that endured were matters of loyalty, duty, and personal honor.

Loyalty to One's Lord

Throughout the ages, loyalty to one's master stands out as an unwavering principle of Bushido. This is understandable since samurai society was a feudal system in which a lord had to have vassals upon whom he could rely unquestionably, and vassals needed the lord's economic support and protection for themselves and their families.

In Japanese feudalism, the master-vassal relationship was exceptionally intense, as exemplified in the story of Torii Mototada. Mototada was a vassal of Tokugawa Ieyasu, a strong samurai warlord under whose leadership Japan was finally unified. During the last decisive days of Ieyasu's drive toward unification, Mototada was placed in charge of Fushimi Castle, where Ieyasu and his troops were garrisoned.

A "Black Sheep" Samurai

All samurai were not shining examples of the code of Bushido, especially in the later centuries when a lot of the glory had diminished. One such ne'er-do-well samurai was Katsu Kokichi (renamed Musui), who wrote down his life story to warn his children and grandchildren not to be like himself. The following excerpt is taken from *Musui's Story: The Autobiography of a Tokugawa Samurai*, translated by Teruko Craig.

"Reflections on My Life

Although I indulged in every manner of folly and nonsense in my lifetime, Heaven seems not to have punished me yet. Here I am, forty-two, sound of health and without a scratch on my body. Some of my friends were beaten to death; others vanished without a trace or suffered one fate or another. I must have been born under a lucky star, the way I did whatever I pleased. No other samurai with such a low stipend spent money as I did. And how I blustered and swaggered about, with a trail of followers at my beck and call!

I wore kimonos of imported silk and fine fabrics that were beyond the reach of most people. . . . I lived life fully. Only recently have I come to my senses and begun to act more like a human being. When I think of my past, my hair stands on end.

He who would call himself a man would do well not to imitate my ways. Any grandchildren or great grandchildren that I may have—let them read carefully what I have set down and take it as a warning. Even putting these words on paper fills me with shame.

I have no learning to speak of, having taught myself to write only in my twenties—and barely enough to cover my own needs at that. My friends were all bad and none good. . . . In everything I was misguided, and I will never know how much anguish I caused my relatives, parents, wife, and children. Even more reprehensible, I behaved most disloyally to my lord and master the shogun and with uttermost defiance to my superiors. Thus did I finally bring myself to this low estate. [He was under house arrest when he wrote his story.]

I am most fortunate in having a filial and obedient son. [His son became a commander in the shogun's army.] My daughters, too, are very devoted. My wife has never gone against my wishes. I am altogether satisfied to have lived until now without any serious mishap. At forty-two I have understood for the first time what it means to follow in the path of righteousness, to serve one's lord and one's father, to live with one's kinsmen in harmony, and to have compassion and love for one's wife, children, and servants.

My past conduct truly fills me with horror. Let my children, their children, and their children's children read this record carefully and savor its meaning. So be it.

Early winter, Tempo 14, The Year of the Tiger (1843)"

When it was discovered that a large enemy force was on its way to attack the castle, it was imperative that General Ieyasu move the bulk of his forces to a more strategic location. However, if the troops were removed, the castle was doomed. Nevertheless, Mototada urged Ieyasu to move his troops, saying that he and his loyal retainers would hold off the enemy as long as possible in order for Ieyasu to regroup his forces.

Not many days after Ieyasu left, the castle was besieged. During the siege, Mototada wrote a long letter to his son in which he eloquently describes what loyalty means to a samurai.

> For myself, I am resolved to make a stand within the castle and to die a quick death. It would not take much trouble to break through a part of their numbers and escape. . . . But that is not the true meaning of being a warrior, and it would be difficult to account as loyalty. . . . It goes without saying that to sacrifice one's life for the sake of his master is an unchanging principle. . . . When I was 13 and Lord Ieyasu seven, I came before his presence for the first time, and the blessings I have received since must not be forgotten for all the generations to come.

> Because Lord Ieyasu is well aware of my loyalty, he has left me in charge of . . . Fushimi Castle while he advances toward the East, and for a warrior there is nothing that could surpass this good fortune. That I should be able to go ahead of all the other warriors of this country and lay down my life for the sake of my master's benevolence is an honor to my family and has been my most fervent desire for many years.[34]

Defenders of the castle were able to hold off the attackers for ten days. At the very last,

unwilling to surrender, Mototada and three hundred samurai repeatedly charged the enemy outside the castle walls. Finally, with only ten men left, Mototada retreated back inside the castle walls. When the enemy soldiers broke through, they graciously allowed Mototada to commit seppuku before taking his head.

The Duty of Vengeance

Closely related to the principle of loyalty to one's master was the necessity to avenge his death if he had been murdered or died through treachery. Samurai vengeance is the theme of one of the most famous stories in Japanese history, that of the forty-seven *ronin*. (Samurai whose masters were deceased or banished were called *ronin*.) In the case of the forty-seven *ronin*, their master, Lord Asano, was ordered to commit seppuku for attacking Lord Kira, a high-ranking officer at the shogun's palace who had publicly humiliated him. Lord Kira's forehead was only scratched in the encounter, and he was not punished for his part in the matter.

Lord Asano's samurai, now *ronin*, felt their master had been treated unfairly and secretly agreed to avenge his death. They made a pact to bide their time until Lord Kira felt safe and let down his guard. Usually in matters of revenge, it was family members of the dead man who did the avenging. Therefore, while Lord Kira was expecting an attack, he was not expecting it from the *ronin*. Almost two years after Lord Asano's death, the forty-seven *ronin* burst into Lord Kira's house and killed him.

Because the incident took place during the peaceful Tokugawa period, the *ronin* were arrested—not because they killed Lord Kira, but because they kept their plans secret. It

The forty-seven ronin *assault the home of the unwary Lord Kira. The story of the forty-seven* ronin's *revenge illustrates how seriously samurai held the notions of loyalty and duty.*

was acceptable to avenge a death as long as prior notice was given to the proper authorities. It was not necessary to say when or where the attack would take place, only that it was intended.

After long deliberation, the ruling shogun sentenced the *ronin* to die by committing seppuku. (Only the youngest of the group was spared.) The decision was not a popular one with the public, as many people felt the *ronin* did what the code of Bushido required, avenged the death of their master. The forty-seven *ronin* became martyred heroes whose story has been told and retold, even in modern films.

Upholding Personal Honor

The matter of the forty-seven *ronin* illustrates another important aspect of Bushido, that of personal honor. Much has been written about this famous case, particularly the motivations of the *ronin*. Since vengeance was ordinarily the business of family members, many writers have speculated on why the *ronin* took

it upon themselves to kill Lord Kira. Eiko Ikegami, author of *The Taming of the Samurai*, writes, "Although they [the *ronin*] talked about personal loyalty to the deceased lord—and their feelings were not hypocritical [insincere]—at the heart of the matter lay the question of their own honor, their own personal sense of pride as well as the [community's] good opinion of them." [35] In the view of the *ronin*, to allow Lord Kira to go unpunished in the death of their lord reflected badly upon them, which, in turn, brought disgrace upon their families.

Samurai were often quick to take offense when they believed their honor had been offended. Personal quarrels and fights (called *kenka*) occurred regularly throughout samurai history, but they were particularly numerous during the peaceful Tokugawa period when samurai had no chance to demonstrate their warrior skills in battle.

Grounds for quarrels were often quite trivial. One story tells of two samurai who were crossing a narrow bridge in the rain when one of them accidentally bumped the other's umbrella with his own. The samurai whose umbrella got bumped felt insulted and called the other an abusive name. Swords were drawn, and the "umbrella offender" was killed on the spot.

The dead man's relatives swore vengeance, but their victim escaped to another province where, by law, he could not be touched. The avengers waited patiently, knowing one day he would get careless and cross the line. When this eventually happened, his ever-watchful avengers were waiting and he was killed in the ensuing sword fight, all over a bumped umbrella. Because they had announced their intentions beforehand, the avengers were not arrested.

"A quarrel provided an important means for vindicating one's position as a samurai," Ikegami writes, "because it was considered a kind of 'mini-battle.' Showing one's back when challenged on the street was as shameful as doing so on the battlefield . . . a quarrel necessitated on-the-spot reactions in defense of one's honor."[36]

The Duty of Seppuku

Another somber obligation of the samurai was accepting responsibility for failure, or for violating some aspect of the warrior's code.

The Tea Ceremony

A widely practiced custom in Japan from early times was the tea ceremony, a serene event that took place within a beautiful setting, often in a special tea house inside a garden. Etiquette was very precise and ritualized. The tea ceremony was very important in the lives of samurai, but, like poetry writing, it was not supposed to become a distracting influence. In *The Code of the Samurai* published in the late seventeenth century, author Daidoji Yuzan gives advice on tea ceremony matters. This excerpt from that work comes from John Newman's *Bushido: The Way of the Warrior.*

"Now as to the tea ceremony. It has always been the great pleasure of the samurai. . . . It may not be necessary to practice it in one's own home, but at least one has to be able to take part in it without embarrassment, when invited for tea at the home of an acquaintance, or when one is on a visit as one of the retinue of a great noble. . . . A samurai needs to have had lessons from a master of the tea, so that he knows at least

how to make the proper movements without drawing attention to himself. . . . The tea ceremony, which aims at sober feeling, is very useful in the cultivation of the Bushido spirit, and a samurai can have made a tea room of his own, very plain in construction, and furnished with new hanging scrolls and new tea cups and an unglazed teapot. However, studied simplicity can often lead to expensive tastes. . . . He may come to feel that he would like better things for himself, and begin to look out where he can pick them up cheaply. . . . In the end he begins to look like a courtier, though his soul is becoming that of a plebeian [common person]; he loses the fundamental spirit of Bushido, and is untrustworthy. So it would be better in that case that he remained a samurai not too well up in the tea ceremony than to become a tea fancier like that. Even if a samurai should happen to become a bit embarrassed about how to behave when he has to serve a cup of tea at a ceremony, still that will not taint his Bushido at all."

Oftentimes, such incidents required samurai to take their own lives in the grim ritual of seppuku, ritual suicide by cutting open one's stomach. This aspect of Bushido evolved through time. The very earliest writings about the samurai did not mention it, and even when it first appeared, it was not the critical matter it later became. Once established, however, seppuku grew into a ritualized obligation undertaken for a variety of reasons.

The original reason for committing seppuku was to preserve personal honor and dignity. Facing defeat in battle and fearful that he might be killed by someone unworthy of his station, a high-ranking samurai took death into his own hands. In situations of personal disgrace, a samurai might choose seppuku to avoid the humiliation of public execution. The courage it took to endure the excruciating pain without flinching erased the dishonor of defeat or disgrace. It also produced some practical results. King explains:

> As a samurai, even though guilty of a death-deserving offense, he could "freely" choose to die by his own hand, in an honorable manner. Thus the disgrace and shame of his deed were erased by his atoning death. Furthermore, it erased his disgrace from the family escutcheon [reputation] and allowed his sons to inherit his name, position, and property; his family as that of a criminal, would have lost its samurai ranking and properties.[37]

In later periods, samurai sometimes used seppuku to protest an unwise course of action taken by their masters or to focus public attention on grave injustices. Such was the case of Suzuki Shigenari, a compassionate samurai official who repeatedly petitioned higher authorities to lessen the tax burden on peasants in his district. When his petitions were ignored, he quit his post and committed seppuku. His selfless act called public attention to the problem, and the tax rate was lowered.

Changes in the Duty of Seppuku

In early times, committing seppuku was a samurai's own decision. There were powerful pressures such as avoiding dishonor or suffering a worse fate at the hands of his enemies, but it was still a warrior's choice. Later in samurai history, seppuku took on legal aspects and was given as a sentence for unpardonable behavior. Under those circumstances, what it really amounted to was execution, albeit an elite one for members of the samurai class only.

The seppuku of Lord Asano is a case in point. He was ordered to commit suicide the same day he attacked Lord Kira, even though a thorough investigation of the matter had not been conducted. Had he not obeyed, he would have been killed by an executioner and his family would have lost their good name and possessions.

Not only did the reasons for but also the customs surrounding seppuku change over the centuries. By the Tokugawa era, the rituals had become very elaborate. A banquet was given for the condemned man at which his favorite foods were served. Many guests were invited for the occasion, and special clothing was worn.

Death by seppuku was so painful that, even in early times, it was acceptable for a samurai to have a swordsman cut off his head shortly after he thrust the dagger into himself. The samurai would give a signal when he wished the swordsman to strike, and stories are told of warriors undergoing extreme pain without complaint before giving the signal.

An image of samurai committing seppuku, or ritualistic suicide. The samurai standing with the sword waits for the kneeling victims to stab themselves before he beheads them.

Few warriors were capable of such feats, however, and by Tokugawa times, it was acceptable to strike off the head of the condemned man just as he reached for the dagger. (This was done in the case of the forty-seven *ronin.*) Sometimes a fan or other symbolic article was substituted for the dagger, making it a pale imitation of the original custom. In spite of these departures from the earlier form of seppuku, King observes:

> Something of the basic dignity of the original form remained: it was a way of death ideally chosen by oneself and by one's own hand, not another's, to atone for some insult given to a higher-ranking person, for some crime committed against others, or for the sullying of the reputation of one's lord or one's family; as one's personal protest against an unjust action or policy; or as a way to move one's lord to a better mode of life [cause him to reconsider an unwise course of action]. It was a final crowning act of freedom and dignity.[38]

Women and Seppuku

Women were not exempt from seppuku, but the occasions for it and the rituals and methods were different from those of men. Sometimes, when the enemy was approaching, women of the household would stab one another

Respected Japanese writer Yukio Mishima committed seppuku in 1970 because he felt the United States was humiliating Japan by keeping the nation demilitarized.

the custom of *junshi,* committing seppuku at the death of one's lord, was prohibited by the shogun in 1664. Nevertheless, noteworthy acts of seppuku continued to be committed into the twentieth century. In 1912 General Nogi, military hero of the Russo-Japanese War, killed himself when his lord and master, Emperor Meiji, died.

As late as 1970 a famous Japanese writer, Yukio Mishima, barricaded himself in the office of a high-ranking Japanese official and committed traditional seppuku. His dramatic act was done to publicly protest the demilitarization of Japan after World War II, which Mishima considered shameful. After stabbing himself in the customary manner, one of Mishima's lieutenants cut off his head.

Leading an Exemplary Personal Life

Although Bushido had a lot to say about death, it also was full of advice about how a samurai should live, both professionally and socially. As professional warriors, samurai were admonished to practice their martial skills unceasingly and to be ready to respond instantly to their master's call. In their domestic lives, samurai were advised to take family duties seriously, respect their parents, and be obedient to them. In his last letter to his son, Torii Mototada wrote, "After I am slain, you must lovingly care for all your younger brothers . . . in my stead. Your younger brothers must earnestly look to you as they would to their father, and must never disobey you."[40]

In addition, a samurai was always supposed to set an example and be a model for others, but since there was no uniform code of Bushido, different writers presented different models. Bushido writers were influenced by ideas and beliefs from many sources

simultaneously, not only to escape being captured but to accompany their husbands in death. Historian Catharina Blomberg writes:

> It was quite common for wives to follow their husbands in death, and this practice, which had no political implications, was never prohibited by law. All *bushi* women carried a knife for the purpose of committing suicide and were instructed from girlhood how to sever the jugular vein. Before doing so, they had to tie their legs together so that their clothing should not be disturbed in an unseemly way in their death-throes.[39]

By the end of the Tokugawa period, seppuku was beginning to be viewed as an unnecessary waste of human life. For instance, including religion (Shinto and Buddhism), philosophy (particularly the writings of the Chinese philosopher Confucius), and the art of war (stories of battles and battle strategy).

Nevertheless, common themes about proper personal conduct occur in all versions of Bushido. These recurring themes are sobriety, simple living, duty to one's lord, obedience to parents, facing death daily without fear, ceaseless practice of the martial arts, the pursuit of learning beyond the martial arts, good manners, and compassion for other people. The differences lie mainly in where the emphasis was placed.

Writers stressing Confucianist principles, for example, tended to emphasize social obligations. Not fearing death was important, but only in that it freed a samurai to carry out his duties more conscientiously. To live a long life was perfectly acceptable. Militant interpretations, on the other hand, laid great stress on duty and death themes. One of the most influential works on Bushido is of this type. Ironically, it was written in the early eighteenth century after all fighting had ceased.

Its author, Yamamoto Tsunetomo, lived during the peaceful Tokugawa era and never participated in combat. His father and grandfather had distinguished war records, however, and Tsunetomo was given a strict military upbringing. In his later years he was extremely distressed to see samurai becoming soft and unprepared in the peacetime atmosphere, so he wrote an eleven-volume work entitled *Hagakure* as a kind of protest. In the opening paragraph of the book he says:

Bushido, or setting the mind in the Way of the Warrior, is nothing strange, yet these days people do not seem to be much concerned with it. In fact, if you ask what they think is the great purpose of Bushido,

The Etiquette of Seppuku

During the Tokugawa period, the custom of suicide by seppuku became so common and so ritualized that passages on how it should be properly done appeared in etiquette books. In this excerpt from *The Taming of the Samurai*, Eiko Ikegami summarizes the advice from one of them.

"One of the most authoritative experts on formal manners during the Tokugawa period, Ise Teijo, gave a list of instructions for the correct preparation of the *seppuku* ritual: the proper manner of taking a bath, as purification before the *seppuku*; the most appropriate hair style; the correct manner of dressing (mostly white), and so on. Teijo goes on to prescribe that the victim's death seat for *seppuku* should be two tatami mats covered by a white sheet. When the man places himself on this death seat, he should first be served with a small ceremonial tray holding two sake cups and a plate holding a collation [light meal]. The manner of serving this food to him, as well as his consumption of it, involved some very complicated points of etiquette. After this food ritual, a ceremonial sword, wrapped with white paper around the middle (as a handle), was placed on a wooden tray in front of him. The *kaishaku* (the headman who decapitated the victim) stood behind the man. Ise Teijo maintains that the remaining details of etiquette can be taught only by oral tradition [presumably because the next steps were too unpleasant for an etiquette book]."

there are few who can give an answer right away. . . . What is called Bushido is simply choosing death. In general, it means that when the moment of decision comes, you simply act so as to die quickly. There are no complications about it. Set yourself firmly, and dash forward.[41]

With no wars going on, this was rather strange advice, but *Hagakure* made a deep impression and continued to influence Japanese militaristic thinking into the twentieth century.

In spite of his preoccupation with death, Tsunetomo also counseled his samurai readers about how to live. His wide-ranging advice included instructions on good manners (never visit someone without previous notice), on raising children (teach boys to be brave and girls to be modest), on proper lifestyles (forsake luxury and do not drink too much wine), and on religion (pray daily).

Most Bushido scholars, including Tsunetomo, believed warriors needed to develop manners and to participate in cultural activi-

Busihdo for Women

Anything that affected samurai warriors also affected the women in their families, and Bushido was no exception. In *Tokugawa Religion: The Cultural Roots of Japan,* author Robert Bellah presents the following passage from a book widely used in the seventeenth and eighteenth centuries to educate samurai women.

"A woman must be ever on the alert and keep a strict watch over her own conduct. In the morning she must rise early, and at night go late to rest. Instead of sleeping in the middle of the day, she must be intent on the duties of her household, and must not weary of weaving, sewing, and spinning. Of tea and wine she must not drink overmuch, nor must she feed her eyes and ears with theatrical performances, ditties, and ballads. . . .

In her capacity of wife, she must keep her husband's household in proper order. If the wife be evil and profligate [wasteful], the house is ruined. In everything she must avoid extravagance, and both with regard to food and raiment must act according to her station in life, and never give way to luxury and pride."

The strict conduct codes of Bushido bled into other aspects of Japanese society, including the role of women. Loyalty and attention to duty were but two of the expectations placed on women.

ties, but there were varying opinions on how far it should go. Daidoji Yuzan, a prominent authority on Bushido prior to Tsunetomo, was more liberal than some, but still cautious. He gives this advice on the popular pastime of poetry writing:

> Now a few words about poetry. To compose poems is a custom of our country. . . . Even a samurai of low rank should be knowledgeable about the art of poetry, and be able to compose a verse himself even though it may well be undistinguished. However, if a samurai gives up everything to plunge into poetry, his heart and even his expression become weak: without realizing it, he gets like one of those courtier samurai . . . and thus he loses his proper warrior's dignity.[42]

Ideal vs. Real

Regardless of which interpretation a samurai adopted, Bushido was basically a set of guidelines by which he could measure his life. It was also an ideal standard that was virtually impossible to follow to the letter. Consequently, samurai frequently fell short of the ideal in everyday life. Blomberg writes:

> Each individual *jusha* [scholar] had his own interpretation of *Bushido,* and although there was a common consensus concerning the key elements of the warrior ethic, opinions differed widely when it came to practical application of the principles. The Confucianists with their training in pragmatism [practical ways] recognized the incontrovertible fact that theory is one thing and practice quite another, and that not everyone can at all times live up to his ideals.[43]

Although they were expected to be ever loyal to their masters, samurai were also supposed to lead exemplary personal lives, showing respect to their wives and families.

Even the principle of complete loyalty to one's master had its limitations. While there was always a core of blood-related relatives in a clan, many samurai had only ceremonial ties to the clans for which they fought. They were hired swords, so to speak, and as such, they expected to be rewarded for their sacrifices.

The Code of Bushido **47**

Whenever a warlord subdued an opponent, he was supposed to share the spoils with his samurai. Discontentment and even defections to other clans occurred if rewards were not forthcoming. Stories of samurai changing sides in the midst of a battle when their side appeared to be losing are common.

When samurai became the elite ruling class of Japan, the Bushido ideal of simple living was shifted to lower class levels. Elite samurai often led lives of luxury and indulgence. Homes of warlords and other high-status samurai were places of great opulence and beauty.

Probably the ideal that was violated more than any other was compassion for others. Even within samurai clans, blood relatives showed no mercy in furthering their own causes. Minamoto Yoritomo owed his military success to his two half-brothers, but when he saw them as threats to his own family's dynasty, he had them hunted down and killed. Vanquished warlords along with their families and allies could expect no mercy. Fire was often used to rout the enemy, and those who tried to escape the flames were killed as they fled, including women and children.

A print of Minamoto Yoritomo slaying a bandit. Although idealized as a great warrior, Yoritomo was not above treachery. Even though his two half-brothers had aided him on his military campaigns, Yoritomo had them killed when he felt they were powerful enough to threaten his family's right to the shogunate.

Poetry and the Samurai

As contradictory as it may seem in the life of a warrior, the composition of poetry was very important to samurai, even in the early eras. Some of the most fierce warlords were also poets who composed verses even when staring in the face of certain death. One of these was Minimato Yorimasa, who, when defeated by the Taira, composed a poem before killing himself. His story, first told in the ancient *Tales of the Heike,* is excerpted from *Cultural Atlas of Japan* by Martin Collcutt, Marius Jansen, and Isao Kumakura.

"Yorimasa summoned Watanabe Chojitsu Tonau [a trusted lieutenant] and ordered, 'Strike off my head.' Tonau could not bring himself to do this while his master was still alive. He wept bitterly. 'How can I do that, my lord?' he replied. 'I can do so only after you have committed suicide.' 'I understand,' said Yorimasa. He turned to the west, joined his palms and chanted 'Hail Amida Buddha' ten times in a loud voice. Then he composed this poem:

> Like a fossil tree
> Which has borne not one blossom
> Sad had been my life
> Sadder still to end my days
> leaving no fruit behind me.

Having spoken these lines, he thrust the point of his sword into his belly, bowed his face to the ground as the blade pierced him through, and died. No ordinary man could compose a poem at such a moment. For Yorimasa, however, the writing of poems had been a constant pleasure since his youth. And so, even at the moment of death, he did not forget. Tonau took up his master's head and, weeping, fastened it to a stone. Then, evading the enemy, he made his way to the river and sank it in a deep place."

In the matter of compassion for the lower classes, the picture is equally grim. For every story of samurai mercy (such as Suzuki Shigenari who died to bring tax relief to peasants), there are hundreds of stories of abuse of commoners. During the Tokugawa period when samurai had the power of life and death over other classes, countless persons were literally cut down on the slightest pretext, usually for not being properly respectful.

In spite of all these deviations, the ideal principles of Bushido influenced the behavior of samurai for centuries in the business of governing the country or administering estates, but especially on the battlefields where so many of them laid down their lives.

CHAPTER 4

The Changing Nature of Combat

Throughout the long history of the samurai class, warriors were involved in many different types of conflicts, even battling armies of discontented warrior monks from militant Buddhist monasteries from time to time. By far the most common type of conflict, however, was interclan fighting, which grew not only more intense in the sixteenth century, but also more widespread as weapons and combat tactics changed.

After Minamoto Yoritomo came to power, he established a stable form of government called the *bakufu*. When Yoritomo died, his widow, Lady Masako, along with members of her own clan (the Hojo family), became the power behind the *bakufu* government.

Acting as regents to the shoguns, the Hojo family ruled behind the scenes for over a century, but were eventually toppled by the Ashikaga clan in 1338. Although the Ashikaga shoguns were literate men and patrons of the arts, they were weak militarily. Moreover, the imperial court had been reduced to a mere figurehead and exerted no authority over civil matters.

Discontented factions and ambitious warlords took advantage of the lack of central authority during Ashikaga rule to advance their causes. Rival samurai clans challenged the ruling shogun, emperors tried to regain authority, and armies of monks, peasants, and townspeople backed by various Buddhist sects rebelled.

Eventually, Japan became a multitude of armed camps hostile to one another and answering to no higher authority. Warrior monks holed up in fortresslike monasteries, and samurai warlords, or daimyo, built castles and other strongholds into which they gathered their families and their samurai retainers and soldiers. During this period, old samurai clans were frequently toppled by brash newcomers.

It was a very different world from the days of individual dueling among relatively small groups of mounted archers. Although cavalry units and corps of trained samurai were still the basis of combat troops, army ranks were now swollen with great numbers of foot soldiers recruited from nonsamurai classes. A new type of battle tactic was necessary, too—that of attacking and defending castles.

Castles for Defense

The type of stronghold a daimyo built obviously depended upon his wealth. Defensive structures of lesser daimyo were actually more forts than castles, while those built by wealthy daimyo were architectural marvels of great beauty and functionality. Japanese castles were of two types: *yamajiro,* those built on hilly sites, and *hirajiro,* those built on plains or in river valleys. During the civil wars of the fifteenth and sixteenth centuries, castles tended to be of the *hirajiro* type in order to protect the daimyo's farmlands.

Great care was taken in the selection of a site to assure a commanding view of the countryside. It was also important to utilize natural defenses, such as rivers in the case of lowland castles or rocky crags for hillside fortresses.

Castle foundations were made of large stones laid over an earthen core. The super-structures of early castles were built of wood, but in later times, stone was used as well. The most striking feature of a wealthy daimyo's castle was the donjon, or central tower rising several stories above the surrounding walls. Delicately curved roofs projecting above each story gave the castle a light, soaring appearance, disguising its more somber purpose. Inside the donjon were residences for the daimyo and his family as well as administrative and military offices.

The donjon was surrounded by an intricate maze of gates, moats, and walls to confuse and obstruct attackers who might be lucky or brave enough to get inside. Some castle complexes were large enough to accommodate thousands of people in times of siege.

In decorating their castles, wealthy samurai warlords completely ignored the Bushido principle of simple living. Lavish furnishings and works of art were poured into them, often to impress those of lesser rank with the importance of the owner. Castles of this sort became cultural and social centers as well as fortresses. Many had theaters and tea ceremony rooms, which were highly fashionable among elite samurai. In his study of the daimyo, Yoshiaki Shimizu describes a castle built by successful warlord Oda Nobunaga:

In 1576 . . . Nobunaga set in motion the building of a magnificent new seven-story castle at Azuchi, overlooking Lake Biwa. Unlike most previous Japanese castles, which were spartan military fortifications, Azuchi Castle was designed to be at once a vast fortress resistant to gunfire, a princely residence, and an impressive stage for

Himeji Castle in Hyogo, Japan, was first constructed by a warrior family in the fourteenth century. Overcoming such permanent defensive structures required a knowledge of siege warfare, a type of combat that was radically different from the man-to-man duels to which the samurai were accustomed.

The Changing Nature of Combat

the public display of political power. . . . Here he could hold lavish ceremonies and entertainments—the castle contained a No stage [a type of Japanese drama], tea ceremony rooms, and a Buddhist chapel—and display his power and majesty to courtiers, daimyo, Buddhist monks, and Christian missionaries who filled its audience chamber.[44]

Castle Towns

Small towns often grew up around castles where farmers, craftsmen, and merchants supplied daimyo and samurai with the necessities of life and the means to defend themselves or conduct campaigns against other samurai. Residence in castle towns was assigned according to rank, with high-status samurai and their families living closest to the daimyo's living quarters. Samurai historian Stephen Turnbull describes a typical castle town arrangement:

Around [the daimyo's] castles, where the family, and some senior retainers lived, were the homes of the other retainers, their distance from the castle walls being in roughly indirect proportion to their rank. The higher retainers . . . were placed just outside the keep, within the castle

Gathering an Army

During the *Sengoku* period when it was every samurai warlord for himself, it often became necessary to draft soldiers in times of emergency. The decree below was issued by daimyo Hojo Ujimasa when preparing to defend his castle against warlord Toyotomi Hideyoshi. The document is excerpted from *Japan: A Documentary History* by David J. Lu.

"Compulsory Military Service
Decreed by Hojo Ujimasa, 1587

1. All men, without distinction as to being of the samurai class or of common people, in this country . . . are ordered to come and register for the service of this province in an emergency. Of these, eight [are to be drafted].

2. They are to bring with them any of the following three weapons: an arrow, spear, or gun. However, a spear, whether its shaft is made of bamboo or wood, is useless if it is shorter than two *ken* [about twelve

feet]. . . . The registration applies to all men from fifteen to seventy years of age.

3. Those who respond to the call must prepare their daggers and military emblems in such a way as to make them look like worthy warriors.

4. If an able-bodied man is deliberately left behind, he and the one who has ordered him to remain will be beheaded immediately by the Minor Deputy . . . of the county upon hearing of it.

5. Anyone who abides by the provisions of this circular diligently, whether he be of the samurai class or of common men, can expect to receive rewards.

The above provisions describe the need in time of emergency. . . . [Instructions on when and how to register follow.] The above provisions must be widely circulated within the county. Fifteenth year of Tensho [1587], last day of the seventh month. To the Minor Deputy and People of Iwase Village."

An image of No performers. Arts, such as No theater, flourished in castles, which, under the protection of daimyo patrons, became cultural centers.

walls proper; the lower were outside the walls, protected perhaps by a moat, or an earthen wall. Completely walled cities on the European model were unknown. Between the two groups of samurai retainers lay the quarters of the favored merchants and artisans, most, if not all, of whom would be engaged in trading and producing the goods that were in demand from the samurai class. Outside the ring of lower samurai lay a quarter of temples and shrines, whose buildings acted as an outer defence cordon, and from where the roads could be sealed off and guarded. From the edge of the castle town began the fields of the farmers, who grew the rice to support those within the [castle town] boundaries.[45]

Castle Warfare

The presence of castles added a new dimension to samurai warfare, calling for both offensive and defensive strategies. Because advancing armies could easily be spotted from castle towers, about the only way to quickly penetrate a castle's defenses was by a swift, unexpected raid before the defenders had time to react. Most of the time, however, castles had to be captured by siege. Attacking armies camped around the castle, sometimes for months, cutting off all incoming food, water, and military supplies until the defenders were starved into submission.

This type of warfare was not especially appealing for rough-and-ready samurai warriors, so castle sieges frequently were

Ninja and Samurai

A mysterious and deadly group of assassins active during the daimyo period were the ninja. They were not samurai, but they were often hired by samurai to kill their enemies by deceit and stealth. In this excerpt from *The Ninja and Their Secret Fighting Art,* author Stephen K. Hayes explains the difference between ninja and samurai.

"Woven into the rich fabric of Japanese cultural, political, and religious history is the story of the incredible art of espionage and individual combat. Its name is *ninjutsu,* the art of stealth, the way of invisibility, and its practitioners were the legendary spies and commandos of feudal Japan known as the *ninja.* Ninjutsu flourished amid the civil turmoil of the fourteenth through seventeenth centuries.

The ninja were commoners, far below the exalted status of the samurai warrior class, and thereby free of the samurai's rigid code of honor and prescribed way of handling situations. The samurai had to balance the dual considerations of achieving his goal and maintaining the honor and prestige of the family name, whereas the ninja was able to concentrate his energy exclusively on the goal at hand, having no honor or name to protect. Because of this total commitment, the service of the ninja commanded a high price.

Women as well as men were trained in the complex art of ninjutsu. *Kunoichi* (female ninja) posing as dancers, entertainers, or servants were often used for observation or espionage inside the enemy camp. Many times female assassins were able to gain the confidence of their victims through beauty and charm when other means of attack had proven futile."

accompanied by attempts to breach the walls and gain entrance to the castle. Defenders had the advantage in these situations by being able to shoot arrows down upon exposed attackers, pour hot liquids on them, or even trick them into disaster, as happened in one castle siege. In this incident, the attacking samurai were able to weaken a portion of a castle wall. Unknown to them, however, the defenders braced up the damaged wall from the inside and lay in wait for the attackers to try to push through. When the attack came, the defenders inside the castle pushed away the braces and toppled tons of stone on the heads of the invaders, killing several hundred of them.

On the other hand, castle attackers had most of the advantages. They could replenish their own troops and supplies while preventing castle defenders from getting reinforcements. All they had to do was wait, but sometimes the fall of a castle could be hastened by ingenuity and a lot of hard work. Fighting in the late sixteenth century to complete the unification of Japan, Toyotomi Hideyoshi and his engineers diverted a river into a castle they were besieging and flooded out the defenders. Ordered to commit seppuku, the defeated general of the castle sailed out into the floodwaters in a boat and killed himself in full sight of Hideyoshi's army.

Sometimes no amount of troops, supplies, or clever tricks could dislodge samurai from their strongholds. Such were the defenders of Chihaya Castle, a mountain stronghold. The defenders, led by samurai Kusunoki Masashige, were loyal to Emperor Daigo, who, early in the fourteenth century, tried to topple the shogun and restore power to the imperial court.

Fighting on his own territory, Masashige and his samurai were able to entice the attackers into indefensible positions. Charge after charge from the shogun's troops were repelled as the defenders shoved boulders on them, dug traps on the pathways, and erected barricades of fallen trees. Though outnumbered, the determined defenders of Chihaya never allowed the castle to be taken.

Preparing for Battle in the Field

Although capturing castles was a vital part of an ambitious warlord's strategy, empires could not be built by castle warfare alone. Sooner or later, armies had to meet on the battlefield. During a century of intense civil wars called the *Sengoku* period (1467–1576), combined clan armies of several thousand warriors were not uncommon.

Moving armies of this size created enormous logistical problems, especially since roads were crude or nonexistent in many places. Moreover, thousands of soldiers had to be fed, clothed, and equipped, and hundreds of horses and pack animals cared for. Such ambitious enterprises called for leaders with extraordinary skills at organization and management as well as at waging war.

Another problem warlords faced was recruitment. In wars of this magnitude, there were not nearly enough samurai to do the fighting, so it was necessary to conscript and train soldiers from other social classes. Weaker daimyo who attached themselves to more powerful ones were obliged to equip and supply a certain number of samurai and foot soldiers for the common army. Trying to meet the conscription quotas without taking away too many of the farmers and artisans to keep their own domains intact was a dilemma faced by many daimyo.

On the March

Once assembled and on the march, a warlord's army presented a brilliant pageant. In the vanguard rode ranks of mounted warriors in superb armor, much changed from earlier days to accommodate new styles of fighting, but still colorful. Mounted on elegant horses, these cavalry troops were accompanied by foot soldiers carrying large, brightly colored standards with the *mons* (family crests) of the clan imprinted upon them.

Hundreds of lower-rank samurai and *ashigaru* in the distinctive colors of their clans followed on foot. Each wore an identifying flag on a long pole attached to the back of his armor. A metal frame across the top held the flag rigid so that its design could be seen at all times. Called *sashimono*, these colorful flags served a very practical purpose of letting generals know where their troops were during combat.

Some *sashimono* had mottoes or even poems printed on them to inspire other samurai. Many flags displayed symbols signifying an idea or object important to the clan represented. The Uesugi clan symbol was a black circle with the outlines of two white lovebirds inside it. Other designs included moons, suns, flowers, Japanese characters (letters), and abstract shapes. A single clan was often represented by several flags, as generals and other high-ranking clan members had their own personal flags.

Before going into battle, daimyo conducted elaborate ceremonies in front of their troops. Although each daimyo had his own traditions, ceremonies always included a review of the troops by the daimyo and his generals, stirring shouts of loyalty from the troops, displays of flags and standards, and prayers and blessings from priests of whatever persuasion the daimyo might be. At the

A painted door panel depicts a mounted samurai in splendid attire. A warlord's army on the march would have been preceded by such horsemen, each carrying the standard of his clan.

conclusion, the magnificently arrayed daimyo would mount his horse and lead the procession to war.

Battle Tactics

A general in the field communicated with his troops in several ways. For example, he might use a handheld war fan to signal his troops to charge, regroup, pull back, or perform whatever action was called for at the moment. However, in large battles where such signals might not be seen, other devices were used, including trumpets made from conch shells, battle drums, and flags. Warriors were trained to understand the messages conveyed by these signaling devices and act accordingly.

The days of challenges and individual duels were long gone. Carefully planned strategy involving large contingents of troops was now the rule. Successful generals were those who tried new, untraditional tactics or

made bold moves. Such a person was Oda Nobunaga, a daimyo from a small province whose military genius led him to fame at a very early age.

Oda Nobunaga first gained prominence in 1560 at the age of twenty-six when he defeated an army of twenty-five thousand men with only three thousand warriors. The defeated leader was Imagawa Yoshimoto, whose wealthy province lay near the Oda clan's domain. Sporadic fighting had gone on between the two clans for years with small fortresslike castles frequently changing hands.

In 1560 Yoshimoto decided he was strong enough to overthrow the weak shogun, a dream cherished by many daimyo. The only thing standing in his way was Nobunaga, but in recent skirmishes with him, Yoshimoto's troops had been victorious. Buoyed up by these successes, Yoshimoto and his army camped in a wooded gorge to celebrate their latest victory over Nobunaga. It was there that the unthinkable happened.

Taking advantage of a sudden violent thunderstorm, Nobunaga and his comparatively small band of men burst upon Yoshimoto's relaxed troops, catching them completely by surprise. Hearing the commotion, Yoshimoto thought some of his men were having a drunken brawl. He very soon realized his mistake when one of Nobunaga's samurai broke into his quarters and killed him after a brief sword fight.

By defeating a much superior force of a prominent daimyo, Oda Nobunaga was on his way to the top. Japanese historian Asao Naohiro says Nobunaga's swift rise to prominence did not happen by chance.

Nobunaga's superior military capacity was not an accident or luck; it was well planned. To facilitate the movement of large forces, he widened and repaired the main strategic roads . . . built pontoon bridges across rivers; and constructed large hundred-oar galleys to transport troops and military gear across Lake Biwa. This made possible the employment of a union of *ashigaru* infantry battalions with the corps of mounted samurai of higher status. And usually Nobunaga was in the lead, whether at the front in a battle or, having decided that the odds were against him, in a swift retreat.[46]

Nobunaga was also famous for his military innovations. Although he was not the first to use the new firearms in battle, he was the first to employ them strategically. "In a battle against a cavalry force, he covered the battlefield with stockades and placed musketeers behind them," writes Henry Wiencek in *The Lords of Japan*. "He organized his musketeers into three groups, two of which loaded their weapons while the other fired at the charging horsemen. The steady fire from the cover of the stockades routed the enemy."[47]

A Shrine for a Shogun

Samurai who reached the exalted position of shogun grandly ignored all the admonitions from the code of Bushido to be frugal and live simple lives. Henry Wiencek, author of *The Lords of Japan*, describes the magnificent shrine Shogun Tokugawa Ieyasu designed for himself.

"The shogun Tokugawa Ieyasu intended his countrymen to revere him forever and toward that end ordered the construction of an awesome temple complex, the Tosho-gu. . . . Over fifteen thousand men—including designers, carpenters, lacquerers, and gilders—labored for twenty years, long after Ieyasu died, building the shrine to a man who considered himself a god.

The construction of the Tosho-gu was no doubt the crowning achievement in the lives of the artists who worked on the shrine. . . . The decoration is so abundant that it hides the basic structures: columns seem less the functional supports of balconies than surfaces around which dragons coil and vines twine. Gleaming lacquer and goldwork adorn much of the basic construction.

Ieyasu died before the Tosho-gu was completed, but in 1617, on the first anniversary of his death, a magnificent cortege—carrying out the shogun's last wishes—delivered his body to the shrine. There his subjects exalted him as the Buddha Incarnate, sun god of the East."

A Unified Japan

In 1582 when Nobunaga was forty-eight years old, he was assassinated by one of his own generals; another of his generals, Toyotomi Hideyoshi, quickly assumed command. Hideyoshi was of humble origins, beginning his military career as an *ashigaru*. He was so capable, however, he was allowed to become a samurai and quickly rose to prominence in Oda Nobunaga's army. In only eight years after Nobunaga's death, Hideyoshi defeated all the warring daimyo and set about establishing a new order in Japan with the samurai class in top position.

Because of his humble origins, Hideyoshi could not take the hereditary title of shogun, which had been passed down through high-ranking samurai families since the days of Yoritomo. However, he was given the title of imperial regent by the emperor, who would not have dared do otherwise.

In 1588, Hideyoshi issued an edict confiscating swords and all other weapons from everyone except the samurai. Although he said the weapons were needed to furnish metal for a magnificent Buddhist statue and temple that he was building, the real reason was to stifle peasant uprisings. Moreover, this action established the samurai as a distinct class, easily recognizable by the two swords only they were allowed to wear in the belts of their flowing robes.

Knowing ambitious samurai clans were as dangerous to central authority as peasant uprisings, Hideyoshi also took stern measures to assure their loyalty. Naohiro explains, "Hideyoshi ordered that the wives and children of the daimyo who submitted to him must live in Kyoto as hostages, while the daimyo themselves were made to serve him in Kyoto with a fixed number of their troops."[48]

Hideyoshi was a master organizer and capable leader in peacetime as well as war, but

Toyotomi Hideyoshi became the military head of Japan in the late–sixteenth century. To ensure his rule would not be upset by rebellion, Hideyoshi disarmed all but the samurai classes and kept all the daimyo's families in the capital as hostages to guarantee loyalty.

Hideyoshi's "Sword Hunt"

In sixteenth-century Japan, farmers made up 80 percent of the population, making peasant uprisings particularly troublesome. To put a stop to rebellions, Imperial Regent Toyotomi Hideyoshi issued a decree for farmers to give up their weapons. To make the confiscation more acceptable, he assured the farmers that it was being done for their own good. The following document is taken from *Japan: A Documentary History* by David J. Lu.

"Collection of Swords, 1588

1. Farmers of all provinces are strictly forbidden to have in their possession any swords, short swords, bows, spears, firearms, or other types of weapons. . . . [The edict gives instructions on who must collect them.]

2. The swords and short swords collected in the above manner will not be wasted. They will be used as nails and bolts in the construction of the Great Image of Buddha. In this way, farmers will benefit not only in this life, but also in the lives to come.

3. If farmers possess only agricultural implements and devote themselves exclusively to cultivating the fields, they and their descendants will prosper. This compassionate concern for the well-being of the farmers is the reason for the issuance of this edict, and such a concern is the foundation for the peace and security of the country and the joy and happiness of all the people. . . . Thus, all the people must abide by the provisions of this edict and understand its intent, and farmers must work diligently in agriculture and sericulture [silk worm production].

All the implements cited above shall be collected and submitted forthwith.

Vermilion seal of Hideyoshi

Sixteenth year of Tensho [1588], seventh month, 8th day."

---

he was also a despot in the strictest sense of the word. He could be extremely cruel to those who displeased him or to anyone who stood in his way. There was even a suspicion that he might be deranged—although no one would have been foolish enough to suggest it out loud. His obsession with wealth led him to build ornate dwellings, including a mansion in Kyoto with a gold-covered roof, and an enormous castle at Osaka filled with art treasures and gold-trimmed furnishings.

"Virtually everything he would have to touch he ordered in gold," Wiencek writes, "his bowls, his chopsticks, the locks on the doors, the latches on the windows. Nothing was exempt from his passion for display. A visitor lamented, 'the very privies are decorated with gold and silver, and paintings in fine colors. All these precious things are used as if they were dirt.' " [49]

In his later years, Hideyoshi decided to invade Korea and sent 150,000 men there in an enormously expensive campaign lasting many years. For a time, his Korean invasion troops were successful, but events soon took a downward turn and a truce had to be arranged. When the truce terms did not suit Hideyoshi, he ordered another invasion. "Loyally, his generals invaded Korea again," Wiencek comments, "and again they met with initial success. After defeating a strong Chinese force, the generals broke off the campaign and returned home when word reached them in 1598 that Hideyoshi had died." [50]

An artist's rendition of the Japanese invasion of Korea. Hideyoshi's campaign was costly in lives and money and was ultimately unsuccessful once China came to Korea's aid.

The Last Samurai Battles

Unlike many samurai leaders, Hideyoshi died a natural death with his head still on his shoulders. Realizing he was dying, he arranged for five regents (all powerful daimyo) to conduct the affairs of state until his only son, five-year-old Hideyori, came of age. Not surprisingly, a power struggle among the regents ensued as soon as Hideyoshi died. It was eventually won by Tokugawa Ieyasu, one of Hideyoshi's most capable generals.

Ieyasu knew he was in no position to act immediately, but being a very patient and shrewd man, he started laying the groundwork for seizing power when the time was

right. His behind-the-scenes maneuvering came to fruition two years later at Sekigahara, a small village on one of the main roads to Kyoto. The decisive battle at that village was the culmination of a fierce military campaign between Ieyasu and his allies and a formidable army composed of his enemies. The battle was the last great struggle between samurai and one of the largest and fiercest conflicts of medieval times. Historian John Whitney Hall describes it:

On the fifteenth day of the ninth month (October 21, 1600), the combined armies of the two factions met in battle at Sekigahara. It is estimated that the eastern league (Ieyasu's faction) committed some seventy thousand men to the engagement. The western league fielded some eighty thousand men, but they were poorly positioned and of uncertain reliability. The battle was in doubt throughout the morning, but the defection of [warlord] Kobayakawa [to Ieyasu's side] turned the tide. Victory went to the eastern coalition.[51]

Being a high-status samurai and claiming descent from the Minamoto clan, Ieyasu had the qualifications to be shogun, a position to which he was duly appointed in 1603. Outwardly, he still supported Hideyoshi's son, Hideyori, who had taken up residence at Osaka Castle, the splendid palace built by his father. As Hideyori grew closer to the age when he would be proclaimed his father's successor, Ieyasu began to plot against him.

Osaka Castle served as the residence of Hideyoshi's son Hideyori. While Hideyori waited to become reigning chief after his father's passing, Tokugawa Ieyasu turned traitor, laid siege to the castle, took the ruling title, and forced Hideyori to commit suicide.

In a trumped-up charge that Hideyori had insulted him, Ieyasu lay siege to Osaka Castle. The first siege against that strong fortress was unsuccessful, but by playing on the fears of Hideyori's mother and by outright trickery, a second siege in 1615 succeeded. The castle was overrun and destroyed. Hideyori and his mother committed suicide and Hideyori's family was murdered. Ieyasu now had no other contenders for control of Japan.

Ieyasu died the following year at the age of seventy-four. His death caused no civil disturbances or clan wars because, during the sixteen years following the Battle of Sekigahara, he had firmly ended daimyo wars and laid the foundations for a stable government. For the next two-and-a-half centuries, shoguns of the Tokugawa lineage maintained peace, during which the lives of the samurai were radically restructured.

Samurai at Home

Although war was a very real fact of life in samurai Japan, the havoc it caused was not total. With only swords, muskets, and a few crude cannon, battles were confined to small areas and did not occur constantly but only periodically.

Living under the threat of war was undoubtedly a great strain, but life went on nevertheless. Samurai married, had families, and lived out their lives in households of various types and sizes. In describing samurai households, two factors must be taken into consideration—the time period in which the household existed and the social rank of the family.

Time Period and Social Rank

The samurai class came into being in the twelfth century because a weakened imperial government left common people unprotected. The first samurai were farmers who put their lands under the protection of a chieftain and served in his private army when the need arose. During the early centuries, loyal samurai were rewarded by their lords with goods and lands confiscated from defeated enemies. The rest of their livelihood came from farming.

At this time, status differences were not as important as they later became, but the

A picture of typical Japanese country people. The samurai class arose from common farmers and townsfolk who served in their village militia.

groundwork was being laid for them. Small chieftains joined with more powerful leaders and a hierarchy of lords and vassals was established. As chiefdoms grew, not only warriors but managers were needed to oversee the affairs of large estates. Some samurai were better at this than others, and status differences began to multiply.

Certain samurai clans such as the Taira and Minamoto rose above others by attaching themselves to the imperial court or making themselves indispensable to it by protecting

House Rules

The fact that all samurai warlords were not insensible or brutish is apparent from the house rules written about 1480 by daimyo Asakura Toshikage. They were addressed to his successor after Toshikage entered a Buddhist monastery. Some of his house rules are excerpted below from *Japan: A Documentary History* by David J. Lu.

"Do not give a command post or an administrative position to anyone who lacks ability, even if his family has served the Asakura family for generations.

Do not excessively covet swords and daggers made by famous masters. Even if you can own a sword or dagger worth 10,000 pieces [monetary value] . . . it can be overcome by 100 spears each worth 100 pieces. Therefore, use the 10,000 pieces to procure 100 spears, and arm 100 men with them. You can in this manner defend yourself in time of war.

Members of the Asakura family must by their own example cause all the retainers to adopt quilted cotton clothing as ceremonial dress at the new Year's celebration. . . . If a member of the family wishes to display his wealth by dressing extravagantly, rural samurai from every corner of this province will be forced to follow suit. However, knowing that [their wealth will not permit them to dress up], they will plead illness and absent themselves from their duties for one year and then for two years. In the end, the number of samurai who pay homage to the Asakura family will be reduced. . . .

When you pass a temple, monastery or town dwelling and the like, rein in your horse for a moment. If the place is attractive, give some words of praise. If the place is damaged, show your concern by expressing your sympathy. These people who consider themselves unworthy will be overjoyed by the fact that you have spoken to them. They will repair the damages expeditiously and pay continued attention to preserve the beauty [of those which you praised]. In this way, without effort on your part, you can keep your province beautiful. Remember that all of these depends upon your resolve. . . .

It will be of no value to you if you take the above articles lightly. I, now a member of a Buddhist order, began my career as a young man and alone. By a determined effort, miraculously I became lord of this domain. Day and night without closing my eyes, I have made plans. . . . I have commanded the soldiers, and now our domain is free from turmoil. If my descendants will adhere to these precepts . . . the province can be preserved and the Asakura name can be maintained."

Unfortunately for the Asakura, they backed the wrong side against Oda Nobunaga and were defeated in 1573, after which Toshikage committed suicide.

A courtier and his attendants. Once the samurai became an elite social class, some held positions in the imperial court while others served as diplomats.

its interests. Through these endeavors, samurai became palace guards, diplomats, courtiers, and eventually even relatives of the emperor by marrying sons and daughters in the royal family. By the time of Minamoto Yoritomo, the first permanent shogun, in the late twelfth century, samurai were already stratified into many social ranks.

In the period of civil wars when castles and castle towns dominated the country (1467–1576), samurai were deliberately cut off from the land. They moved into castle towns to serve daimyo as full-time warriors and retainers while the farming was left to another class of people considered beneath the standing of samurai.

In the peaceful Tokugawa period after unification (1603–1853), these distinctions became even greater. Only samurai were allowed to have weapons, and their superiority over other classes was written into law. Since they now had no other means of livelihood, samurai received stipends, or fixed salaries, from the daimyo in whose domain they resided. The amount they received was based upon their social rank.

In return, samurai families were expected to serve the daimyo in a number of ways, and to maintain a standard of living corresponding to the stipend they received. Such matters were not left to the discretion of the recipient but were dictated by the ruling daimyo even to the number of horses and servants a household must maintain and the kind of clothes the family could or could not wear.

High-ranking samurai managed fairly well, but many lower-class families were so poor they often had to swallow their samurai pride and take menial jobs. Historian Teruko Craig comments, "They supplemented their meager stipends by making toys, lanterns, and umbrellas or by working as carpenters, plasterers, and gatekeepers."[52]

All families walked a tightrope, however, in that a family of any rank might lose its stipend or have it reduced if the family did not live up to expectations. Many samurai families of this era outwardly seemed prosperous but struggled behind the scenes to maintain their positions.

A Diplomatic Letter to a Daimyo

Tokugawa Nariaki, daimyo of Mito province, decided that one of his favorite retainers, Aoyama Isamu, should be married to the daughter of a prominent family. As samurai marriages were arranged by parents, Nariaki ordered Isamu's father, Aoyama Enko, to start negotiations with the girl's family. Isamu did not approve of Nariaki's choice for his bride and appealed to his father, who wrote the following letter to Nariaki excerpted from *Women of the Mito Domain* by Yamakawa Kikue.

"Having received your command concerning a wife for Isamu, I looked into the matter of Takeda's granddaughter and learned that she is a very tiny person, so much so that although she is seventeen years old, she looks more like a child of twelve or thirteen, and does not appear at all of an age to marry. Her attitude, too, seems very childlike. . . . Since

everyone thinks her to be no more than twelve or thirteen, people would find it strange were she suddenly to take on the appearance of a young wife. It would be awkward to introduce her to others as one's wife since in physical appearance she would seem more like a little sister. For these reasons her parents, too, say that for the moment they do not intend to marry her to anyone. . . . The circumstances being such, I regret that a formal proposal does not seem appropriate; thus I have not made one."

Enko then wrote the following to his son.

"He accepted my objection that she is exceedingly small. . . . Since his lordship has commanded you that you should choose a wife from among the circle of the committed [loyal families], the task of finding one will not be easy."

Obviously, there were great differences in lifestyles among samurai, but there was also a core of common practices in all time periods and social ranks. These common themes included family structure, marriage, household management, family roles, fashions, and amusements.

Family Structure

The core of a samurai family was a group of members related by blood or marriage, but unrelated persons could also be included. Historian Mikiso Hane writes, "The family was the essential unit upon which the feudal relationship was constructed. The samurai built his power structure by extending his family ties to all his blood relations, enlarging it further by marriage connections, and encompassing followers. Such a follower was virtually regarded as a family member and called 'a man of the house'. . . or a 'child of the house.'"[53]

Primogeniture was the rule in samurai families, meaning the oldest son inherited his father's role and became head of the family at his father's death or retirement. This left younger sons in a bad position, particularly in the Tokugawa era when there were no wars to occupy them and not enough government positions worthy of their status to go around. It was therefore the practice of samurai families to adopt younger sons of other families, especially if there was no son of their own to inherit.

Writing about her own samurai ancestors, Yamakawa Kikue says of this practice, "An inheriting daughter without any brothers had no trouble finding a husband, for there were any number of younger sons whose only opportunity to become a full-fledged member of society rested upon being adopted into another house."[54]

Because of early marriages and high birthrates, samurai households often had as many as three generations living together. Fringe relatives such as uncles, aunts, or cousins whose own homes had been disrupted for one reason or another often took up residence in a related samurai household.

Samurai Marriage

When the imperial court was at its peak before the samurai emerged, women enjoyed high status. (At least those of high rank did. Not very much is known about how the common people of this era lived.) A prominent writer of that period was Sei Shonagon, a lady-in-waiting at the imperial court. Commenting in her diary about court women, she writes:

> Women at Court do not spend their time modestly behind fans and screens, but walk about, looking openly at people they chance to meet. Yes, they see everyone face to face, not only ladies-in-waiting like themselves, but even Their Imperial Majesties (whose august names I hardly dare mention), High Court Nobles, senior courtiers, and other gentlemen of high rank. In the presence of such exalted personages the women in the palace are all equally brazen.[55]

With the ascendancy of the samurai, this kind of freedom for women ended. In the strict military protocol of warrior palaces and households, women had little to say about their own lives. Marriages were arranged by parents and elders, and mates were selected to further the interests of the clan. In the higher ranks of samurai, this was especially true.

An example is that of O-ichi, sister of warlord Oda Nobunaga. O-ichi's first marriage to Shibata Katsuie, a high-ranking official, was arranged by her brother. However, when Nobunaga needed to form an alliance with another clan, he commanded O-ichi to divorce Katsuie and marry the heir of the clan he wanted as an ally. When this alliance turned sour, O-ichi's new husband sent her back, and Nobunaga ordered her to remarry Katsuie. After Nobunaga was murdered, Katsuie opposed General Hideyoshi's move to take over the reins of government. When Hideyoshi won the power struggle, O-ichi was forced to end her troubled life by committing suicide along with her husband.

Marriage Customs

Marriages were arranged for the clan's benefit in lower-class samurai families as well, and neither bride nor bridegroom had a lot to say about the arrangements. Nevertheless, both men and women sometimes found ways of getting out of a marriage arrangement they considered wholly unsuitable. Such was the case of Aoyama Isamu, a young samurai who was selected to serve at the daimyo's residence in Edo.

The daimyo, Tokugawa Nariaki, took a personal interest in Isamu and decided that he needed a wife. This in itself was not unusual, but when Isamu learned the identity of the prospective bride Nariaki had chosen, he was horrified. She was not at all the kind of person he wanted for a wife. In desperation, he wrote a letter to his father asking him to try and dissuade Nariaki.

This was a delicate matter as one simply did not refuse a daimyo's orders. However, in a diplomatically worded letter to Nariaki, Isamu's father suggested that the girl was not the type who would make the clan proud when presented at Edo social functions. This subtle appeal to clan pride did the trick and Nariaki backed off. However, if he had insisted, Isamu and his family (as well as the young lady and her family) would have been compelled to comply as obedient vassals of their lord.

In matters of relations with the opposite sex, samurai men had much greater freedom than women. Some well-to-do samurai households included concubines, women who acted as surrogate wives and bore children fathered by the master of the household. The official reason given for this practice was to assure a male heir to carry on the family name, but in effect, it simply gave men a sexual outlet that women did not have.

As a whole, samurai women accepted the presence of concubines, having observed the practice from an early age and having been taught to expect it in their own marriages. Wives even had the right to approve concubines before they were brought into the household. However, when a concubine came to have a more favored position than a wife, as sometimes happened, household harmony was seriously disrupted. Since the keeping of concubines was only possible in wealthier households, it was not a big problem for the majority of samurai families.

Men were favored in other ways, too. If a wife strayed from her marriage vows, both she and her paramour could be killed on the spot, but husbands were free to have affairs (other than with concubines) as long as the women they pursued were not married. Many

samurai men were bisexual, as well, particularly in the early days when they were often away on military assignments. Male sexual partners were not uncommon, nor was such a relationship considered immoral.

Samurai Divorce

Divorce, like marriage, was handled by parents and elders. Based on the teachings of Confucius, there were seven reasons a man could divorce his wife: disobedience to in-laws, failing to bear children, lewdness, having leprosy or other terrible disease, jealousy, causing trouble by talking and gossiping too much, and stealing.

For women, getting out of an intolerable marriage was more difficult. Under some circumstances, she might return to her parents' home, but such situations were socially very awkward. When a situation became intolerable, ever-watchful relatives or domain leaders would step in. Yamakawa Kikue writes:

> Had there not been such intervention by the domain or relatives or had common sense and natural human feelings not served to limit excessive self-indulgence on the part of men, women of this age would indeed have lived in a mire of constant misery. While women were subject to severe pressures in the name of the house, however, the position of the wife was protected and to a certain degree stabilized also in the name of the house.[56]

While there were doubtless many happy marriages and devoted couples among the samurai, the prevailing attitude toward women and marriage voiced by daimyo Tokugawa Nariaki was all too common. He wrote to one of his vassals that it was acceptable for high-born people like himself to have many wives and children, but not for those of low status. In his letter, he concluded, "The sole function of women is to bear children. . . . Other than that everything they do can be done by a man. . . . In short, the only function a woman serves is to increase one's progeny."[57]

The Samurai Household

Once married, middle- and lower-class samurai women were largely confined to the home, and their days were filled with domestic chores, caring for children, and managing the household according to exacting samurai standards. Women rarely traveled and were not told about events going on in the outside world.

Due to the wide range of social classes, samurai dwellings ranged from crude hovels with few amenities to palatial mansions with lavishly decorated interiors, tea houses, and extensive gardens. In between those extremes, samurai homes tended to be traditional middle-class Japanese residences with two main areas, described by historian Susan B. Hanley:

By the Tokugawa period, virtually every house that was not a mere hovel was divided into two parts: a "living" area and a "service" (or work) area. The service area was used for preparing meals, as a workplace, and for storage. Privies and stables were a part of the service area, and often all were under the same roof. The floor of the service area in every house (the *doma*), no matter how wealthy the occupants, was invariably packed earth, though it was an integral part of the house. The floors of living rooms were made of boards, split bamboo, or tatami

A Traditional Samurai Wedding

Born into a samurai family in the late nineteenth century, Yamakawa Kikue writes about life in samurai households of the Tokugawa period in *Women of the Mito Domain: Recollections of Samurai Family Life*. In the following passage, she describes a traditional wedding witnessed by her mother, Chise, when she was a child.

"Chise saw only one traditional bridal procession. The occasion was the marriage of her cousin, the current head of the Sekiguchi family. The bride came to the Sekiguchi house in a palanquin [an enclosed seat attached to poles and carried on the shoulders of two or four men] following the bridegroom, who, dressed in stiff hempen *kamishimo*, rode on horseback.

Over an underrobe of pure white the bride wore a kimono of scarlet crepe with a narrow pink satin obi and a long loose overrobe of blue-gray embroidered in gold and silver from top to bottom with a pattern of cartwheels. The bridal attendant from the groom's side, Yoshinari Yuki, was dressed in blue-gray crepe with an overrobe embroidered around the hem. The bride's mother and the attendants from her side all wore overrobes, too. The seventeen-year-old bride, glimpsed by the light of a lantern flickering against a gold screen, was indeed like a flower in full bloom. Her hair, under the bride's hairdress, was done up in a matron's *marumage* [upswept hairdo worn only by married or about-to-be-married women]."

Middle-class samurai women were wedded to a domestic life. The requirements of their social position kept them inside their homes without much contact with the outside world.

[reed mats], or a combination of these in houses that had raised flooring. In those houses in which flooring was beyond the family means, the living section of the dwelling was separated from the work area by a sill, and the ground was covered with husks, hulls, and straw which were then covered with straw mats for sitting and sleeping.[58]

Samurai houses were usually one-story dwellings with an entry gate and an entrance hall to receive guests. Other rooms off the main area were connected by corridors, often winding back and forth. Since the beauty of nature was highly prized, most samurai homes had attractive gardens that could be viewed from the living areas. Because the roof was supported by posts instead of load-bearing walls, sliding partitions provided privacy or spaciousness as needed. This flexibility and openness was fine in summer, but samurai houses were often miserably cold in winter.

Samurai homes had only a few furnishings such as chests, low tables, and desks. There were no chairs, but there might be an armrest to lean on while sitting on the floor. Family members slept on the floor on heavy mats that were rolled up and stored out of the way during the day. Decorations were wall scrolls and perhaps a simple flower arrangement in a special alcove. Light was provided by lanterns.

Food was prepared on open braziers or in a large pot over a fire pit built on the clay floor. In high-status families, meals were eaten from individual trays, with family members all eating at the same time, conversing and enjoying one another's company.

Samurai Diet

The amount and variety of foods served depended upon the family's financial situation. The main staple was rice, supplemented with soups, vegetables, eggs, and a variety of pickled foods. Potatoes, both white and sweet, were introduced in the sixteenth century and were credited with reducing the death toll from terrible famines that periodically occurred when the rice crop failed.

A woman offers a cup of sake to a group of nobles. Sake was the preferred alcoholic beverage in early Japan, though it was not affordable for many lower income families.

Even though rice remained the staple food throughout the centuries, other less expensive grains such as barley and millet were often substituted in low-income families. Since most samurai were Buddhists, meat was rarely eaten, but fish, either fresh or dried, was acceptable fare. There were fruits, too, such as peaches, pears, and plums. Rice cakes and rice dumplings were special treats served occasionally. Tea was the preferred drink, and sake, or rice wine, was the favorite alcoholic beverage.

Family Roles

Family roles were based on Confucian principles and rigidly defined. Hane comments:

> The father was at the top of the family hierarchy and held absolute authority. Filial piety [devotion to parents] was a virtue prized equally with loyalty to the lord. It was a moral ideal upheld by all thinkers and embraced by all segments of the society. There was, in addition, a hierarchy of age and sex. The younger brother had to defer to the older brother and women to men. . . . A samurai's wife was to be absolutely obedient to her husband and serve without any complaints, enduring all forms of hardship and abuse.[59]

Particularly in the early centuries, however, men were away at war a lot of the time so women had to shoulder responsibility for managing the household. As women grew older, they had much more to say about family matters, especially those affecting household management and the marriage of their children. The role of a new bride, on the other hand, was a particularly difficult one.

Still in her teens, she moved into her husband's household where her mother-in-law was firmly in charge.

Except for women in the wealthiest samurai homes, wives, daughters, and other female members of a household did a great deal of the work themselves. Although there were sometimes maids and other servants to help (depending upon the rank of the family), samurai women not only prepared food for the family but oftentimes helped grow it. They also made all the clothing, from spinning the thread to making the finished garment.

In spite of their subordinate status, samurai women as a rule were not timid or weak, nor were they intended to be. They were taught from an early age to defend themselves and were trained in the use of the *naginata*. Japanese chronicles tell of women who fought to the end alongside their husbands, fathers, and sons when attacked in their home or castle.

Toddlers were given a great deal of love and attention, but obedience and manners were stressed at an early age. Lives of boys and girls were similar until they were about six or seven, when martial arts began to be emphasized for boys and household duties for girls. Both were taught basic reading and writing skills, at least in later, more prosperous samurai families. However, formal education was considered much more important for boys than for girls.

Fashions and Social Customs

Although samurai warriors had only scorn for fancily dressed men of the imperial court, they too had a fondness for style judging from their colorful armor and elaborate helmets. This tendency carried over into their private lives as well. By the Tokugawa period, samurai men were clearly identified by the clothes they wore and by their hairstyle.

Pictures of early samurai warriors often show them with wild, unkempt hair, but gradually a distinctive hairstyle developed. A samurai's hair was trimmed close to his head in

A samurai surrounded by the women of his household. Samurai women performed all of the domestic chores such as cooking, tailoring, and caring for the children. They were also taught self-defense in case the samurai home was invaded.

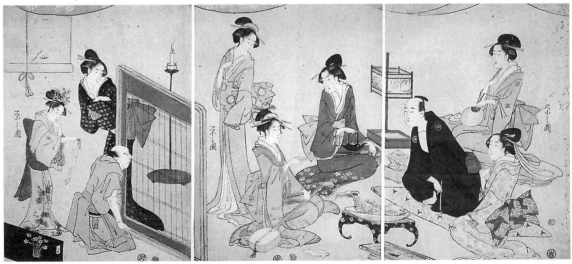

A Samurai Boy Comes of Age

A samurai boy officially became a man at the age of fifteen or sixteen in a ceremony called *genbuku*. Catharina Blomberg describes this coming-of-age rite in *The Heart of the Warrior,* from which the following passage is excerpted.

"The son of a *bushi* [samurai] was initiated in his future warrior status at the age of six or seven, when the ceremony of *yoroi-kizome,* the first wearing of armor, was celebrated, whereas his coming of age ceremony, *genbuku,* was a much more solemn occasion. The *genbuku* was usually celebrated at the age of fifteen or sixteen, when the young samurai was considered an adult man, and it took the form of a solitary vigil during a night spent in a Buddhist temple. In the morning the young man was dressed in the formal robes of an adult *bushi,* and his *eboshi-oya* [hat godfather] usually an older male relation or friend of the family who held a senior position, tied on the young man's *eboshi,* the stiff black gauze hat traditionally worn with the formal costume of the Heian court, for the first time. In the Heian period the young man also had his teeth dyed black for the first time on this occasion."

front, and the top of his head was shaved. The hair in back was allowed to grow long so that it could be caught up in a pigtail, oiled, and lapped back over the shaved portion of the head. It was held in place with pomade, a kind of sticky ointment. Keeping it in place was difficult and sometimes it had to be redone during the day. A boy was not allowed to wear a man's hairstyle until he was fifteen or sixteen and ready to undergo *genbuku,* a solemn coming-of-age ritual.

Clothing worn by samurai men also set them apart. Formal dress, known as *kamishimo,* consisted of a pair of wide-legged trousers called *hakama* and a matching jacket with wide, stiffened shoulders. Both of these garments were worn over a kimono. On less formal occasions, he might wear a loose jacket (*haori*) over a kimono and *hakama.* On his feet were wooden sandals (*geta*) worn with cotton socks (*tabi*). *Tabi* were made with a separate slot for the big toe to accommodate the sandal thong. The ensemble was completed with the most impressive samurai symbols of all, a long and a short sword stuck into his belt.

Samurai women dressed according to their position in the social ranking system. In less wealthy households, all the clothing, men's included, was made by the women of the household from start to finish, mostly from cotton, as silk was more difficult to produce. This process included spinning cotton or silk into thread, weaving it into cloth, dying the cloth, and sewing the finished garments. Young samurai girls started learning to sew at the age of twelve, often at special schools run by impoverished samurai women. Although in later centuries clothing could be purchased in stores, many samurai families living on fixed incomes could not afford such luxuries.

The traditional dress for a woman was a kimono tied at the waist with a sash called an obi. While she was working, the full sleeves of the kimono were tied back out of the way. Kimonos varied in pattern and fabric according to the rank and wealth of the household. In poorer families, kimonos were hard to come by and carefully preserved, as Yamakawa Kikue relates:

Since to make a new piece of clothing was a major undertaking, a woman was expected to take the best care she could of the clothes she had so as to pass them on in good condition to her daughters and granddaughters. In fact, since they only rarely left the house, women probably had little opportunity to wear anything other than ordinary dress. For them, good kimono were something to keep than to wear. But there were certain things it was essential to have, such as clothes to wear to a wedding or a funeral. In those days when one couldn't run at the last minute to a department store or a rental clothes shop, bushi [samurai] women were expected to possess an appropriate range of clothing, even if they only wore it very rarely.[60]

The elaborate hairstyles of Japanese women were held in place with a variety of decorative ribbons and pins.

A Japanese girl dressed in a kimono that is tied at the waist with an obi. The material and pattern of a kimono indicated the social status of the wearer's family.

Hairstyles were as important to samurai women as to men and were also governed by age and custom. A little girl's hair was cut in bangs, braided, or shaved leaving a little top-knot. As they grew older, girls let their hair grow so that by the time they were ready to marry at about fifteen or sixteen, they had learned the basics of doing their hair as married women did. However, it took a long time to become skillful at creating the fashionable pompadour hairstyles dictated by fashion.

Other fashion customs followed by girls at marriage were shaving off their eyebrows and blackening their teeth. Bushy eyebrows were considered uncouth and white teeth were felt to be unsightly. Teeth were stained with a dye made from natural substances. In earlier days, even warriors blackened their teeth, but the custom died out among men, except for those in the imperial court.

Amusements

The ways in which elite samurai amused themselves, such as collecting artworks, hosting elaborate parties, or building tea houses, were available only to those who had wealth and leisure time. For example, at the time when Japan was undergoing the worst of its civil wars, Shogun Ashikaga Yoshimasa (1436–1490) withdrew into his own luxurious world and refused to deal with, or even acknowledge, the strife going on around him. Henry Wiencek writes in *The Lords of Japan:*

> In one of the darkest hours of Japanese history, when civil war threw the country into a tumult, Japan's military ruler, Shogun Yoshimasa, spent his days composing poetry, presiding over lavish court fetes, and viewing paintings and antique porcelain. Fouding lords reduced the country side to ashes, and the long-smoldering grievances of the peasants erupted into rioting and pillage. Meanwhile the shogun meditated in his gardens and designed new palaces.[61]

Though life was often grim for ordinary samurai, there were still diversions from daily duties. Board games were popular. A scene from an old woodblock print shows samurai relaxing in a castle, polishing their swords and playing go, a game of strategy between two players that is somewhat like chess. Two other samurai in the picture who seem to be enjoying themselves are playing *sugoroku* (similar to backgammon).

Music was also a popular diversion, played on stringed instruments and flutes. For the elite, No dramas, theatrical performances combining music, dancing, masks, and magnificent costumes, were available. Kabuki theaters were popular with the common people, although samurai were not encouraged to attend. Kabuki theaters presented plays about Japanese folk heroes, and Kabuki actors became popular idols among all classes.

When the *bakufu* decreed that women could no longer take part in Kabuki plays, men dressed up as women and the plays became more popular than ever. Historians Martin Collcutt, Marius Jansen, and Isao Kumakura write, "Samurai were officially discouraged from wasting time or money on such frivolous pursuits but they, no less than other sections of the population, were drawn to the theaters."[62]

Samurai in the large cities were also drawn to less savory amusements such as gambling, drinking, and prostitution. Since bakufu

A woodcut of a Kabuki actor in an ornate costume. Male Kabuki actors portrayed both male and female characters since women were barred from taking part in the theater.

officials found it impossible to stamp out these activities, they confined them to certain areas of the city. These "licensed areas" existed mainly for townspeople, but by the end of the Tokugawa period, a large percentage of the patrons were samurai.

Children's Amusements

Children's amusements were similar to those of children in all times and places, including toys, dolls, ball games, kites, singing activities, active outdoor games, and card games. Festivals were a favorite among children as well.

Samurai descendant Yamakawa Kikue describes a festival at a school attended by her mother when she was a young girl.

On the twenty-fifth of the second and eleventh months the school held a festival in honor of Sugawara no Michizane [patron deity of scholarship]. . . . The students hung lanterns along both sides of the path leading from the school to the shrine. . . . Each lantern was decorated with a Chinese or Japanese poem or a picture. . . . Next to the shrine, banners inscribed by the students fluttered in the breeze, and on a makeshift platform a

---

The No Drama

As ruthless as they may have been in battle, samurai were also patrons of the arts. Shogun Tokugawa Ieyasu, for example, was so devoted to the No drama that he made it the official theater of Japan. Henry Wiencek describes the wonders of the No drama in this excerpt from *The Lords of Japan.*

"Upon the simplest of stages, before the most aristocratic of audiences, Japanese actors and musicians perfected one of the truly unique forms of theater in the world, the solemn No drama. No, meaning 'accomplishment,' combined mime, dance, chant, music and especially costume into an otherworldly experience that surpassed being mere entertainment to powerful military families of the sixteenth century. For after Shogun Tokugawa Ieyasu decreed it the official theater of Japan, performances of the elegant, rarefied No—which had actually begun in the fourteenth century—

constituted great state occasions. Prominent families of the time actually studied No themselves and patronized it by building stages in their mansions and supporting troupes of actors. . . .

Since the stage is essentially bare, the performers' robes and masks are more like sets than costumes and are crucial to the unfolding of the drama. . . . The masks, sculpted of Japanese cypress, represent idealized personalities of both human and superhuman characters and each has its own name. . . . No robes are among the supreme achievements of the textile arts, usually made of silk brocades, satins, and gauzes. . . .

The privileged members of the Tokugawa society loved the No, rewarding those actors and musicians who gave them pleasure—and punishing those who failed to do so. The unfortunate actor who misstepped or musician who misplayed in performance might be banished."

Music was a common diversion for samurai families. Here, a small group relaxes while two women pluck traditional stringed instruments.

drum was set up which they proceeded to beat noisily throughout the night.[63]

Both children and adults delighted in nature, and the blossoming of plum and cherry trees in the spring was the occasion for many festivals and outings. Cherry and plum blossoms were a favorite theme for samurai poets who likened their own precarious lives to the swift passing of the blossoms.

As important as amusements and diversions were throughout the centuries of samurai rule, they became even more necessary in the peaceful Tokugawa period when many samurai found themselves with dwindling resources and time on their hands.

Samurai in Peacetime

In feudal Japan, the death of a strong leader usually signaled a new round of fighting among rival samurai clans. Shogun Tokugawa Ieyasu ended that. Appointed shogun in 1603, he established an orderly government with stern measures to curb the power of the daimyo. Several years before his death at the age of seventy-four, Ieyasu resigned as shogun so that his son could assume the position and be firmly in power when Ieyasu died. The plan worked exceedingly well, as members of the Tokugawa lineage ruled for 250 years.

Dutch emissaries are granted an audience with Tokugawa Ieyasu. The shogun expelled most Europeans from Japan during the Tokugawa era, yet a few Dutch traders were permitted to stay.

Peace among the daimyo was enforced with an iron hand during the Tokugawa era. The imperial court and Buddhist monasteries were treated with respect, but their activities, too, were closely monitored and controlled. Moreover, Ieyasu started Japan on a strict policy of cultural isolation. Foreigners, including Christian missionaries who had begun making converts, even among the samurai, were expelled or killed. Japanese citizens were forbidden to travel outside the country and only a few Chinese and Dutch traders were allowed to remain inside Japan near the port city of Nagasaki.

As strong as the new peacetime government was, however, there were vast new problems confronting it, not the least of which was what to do with thousands of samurai warriors and their families when there were no battles to fight.

Tokugawa Social Structure

Based on the teachings of Confucius, Tokugawa social structure consisted of four major divisions. At the top were warriors, followed by peasants who raised the food that sustained the entire system. Next were artisans, creators of goods for war and domestic uses. At the very bottom of the scale were merchants. While the goods and services they provided were necessary, merchants themselves were thought to be greedy and dishonorable.

Closing the Country

Beginning in the seventeenth century, Japan's leaders began to impose a state of isolation upon the country, expelling foreigners and refusing to allow Japanese to travel outside the country. The crackdown was especially severe on Christian missionaries and their converts, as shown in the following edict taken from *Japan: A Documentary History* by David J. Lu.

"The Edict of 1635 Ordering the Closing of Japan: Addressed to the Joint Bugyo [city officials] of Nagasaki

1. Japanese ships are strictly forbidden to leave for foreign countries.

2. No Japanese is permitted to go abroad. If there is anyone who attempts to do so secretly, he must be executed. The ship so involved must be impounded and its owner arrested, and the matter must be reported to the higher authority.

3. If any Japanese returns from overseas after residing there, he must be put to death.

4. If there is any place where the teachings of padres [Christianity] is practiced, the two of you must order a thorough investigation.

5. Any informer revealing the whereabouts of the followers of padres [Christians] must be rewarded accordingly. If anyone reveals the whereabouts of a high ranking padre, he must be given 100 pieces of silver. For those of lower ranks, depending upon the deed, the reward must be set accordingly.

6. If a foreign ship has an objection [to the measures adopted] and it becomes necessary to report the matter to Edo, you may ask the Omura domain to provide ships to guard the foreign ship, as was done previously.

7. If there are any Southern Barbarians [Westerners] who propagate the teachings of padres, or otherwise commit crimes, they may be incarcerated in the prison maintained by the Omura domain, as was done previously.

8. All incoming ships must be carefully searched for the followers of padres."

A number of additional rules pertain to the distribution of goods brought into Japan by approved traders.

The four classes were split into dozens of subclasses with rigid rules and little crossing of lines. This was especially true of the samurai. Historian Mikiso Hane writes, "A nineteenth-century intellectual leader, Fukuzawa Yukichi, who came from a small han [domain] in northern Kyushu, reported that there were more than one hundred different degrees of rank in his han where there were only fifteen hundred samurai. Proper distinctions of status were maintained at all levels."[64]

By Tokugawa times, political circumstances, much of them deliberate, had gradually separated the samurai from other classes. Edicts requiring samurai to live in special areas in cities or castle towns set them apart geographically. Allowing only samurai to possess weapons and granting them power over commoners set them apart socially. While the code of Bushido advised samurai to use compassion in dealing with members of the lower classes, many of them ignored the advice and became arrogant bullies.

Historians Martin Collcutt, Marius Jansen, and Isao Kumakura explain, "Commoners feared samurai. Even a poor samurai would show disdain for a wealthy merchant or substantial farmer. When *daimyo* processions passed along the roads to and from Edo, commoners had to step aside and kneel in the dust."[65] Those who did not pay respects could be killed on the spot with the samurai's *katana*. There are even stories of samurai ambushing peasants on rural roads just to test the killing power of new swords.

Commoners were not totally defenseless, however. Swords and other weapons could be obtained illegally, and many methods of self-defense without weapons were widely known and practiced. In cities and towns, vigilante-like groups banded together to protect themselves against unprincipled samurai.

Making a Living in Peacetime

Although civil disturbances still erupted occasionally (usually led by overburdened peasants), there was little need for the services of fighting men in Tokugawa times. The result was a great many samurai without full-time jobs. As bad as the situation was, it might have been worse had Ieyasu not been a gifted statesman as well as a military leader. After his victory, he spared the lives of opposing daimyo, not out of compassion, but because he needed them. Recognizing the effectiveness of the daimyo management system (he had been a daimyo himself), he allowed the basic structure to remain. This decision assured the continued livelihood of many samurai as retainers, managers, and workers in the domains.

Ieyasu did reassign daimyo to different territories, however. Those who supported him were rewarded with lucrative provinces close to the capital city of Edo while his opponents were sent to manage provinces in outlying areas of the country. To further assure their subservience, opposing daimyo were required to sign loyalty oaths and their provinces were carefully watched by loyal daimyo whose domains were situated on their borders.

Samurai were paid stipends for their services by the daimyo whom they served, the amount being based on position and social rank. The basic monetary unit in Japan was one *koku*, the amount of rice to sustain a man for one year (approximately 5.1 bushels). Stipends ranged from less than a hundred *koku* for the lowest ranks of samurai to thousands of *koku* for the very highest positions. Payment could be in actual bales of rice, or when currency began to be used, in an equivalent amount of money.

Since daimyo were held responsible for the efficient management of their domains, they were constantly issuing directives to their samurai retainers about being thrifty. In her recollections of samurai life, Yamakawa Kikue tells of an austerity program initiated by Tokugawa Nariaki, head of the Mito domain. In an effort to cut back on domain expenses, he forbade his vassals to display flower arrangements, to keep or play musical instruments, or to perform the tea ceremony. He also issued an edict restricting the wearing of silk, which reads as follows:

Item: His lordship has heard that in recent years customs have grown exceedingly extravagant, with people drawn to what is splendorous and losing a sense of sobriety. Thus he is ordering all his retainers to wear clothes made of cotton.

Item: Those above the rank of samurai may wear undergarments [robes worn under a kimono] made of silk or pongee [thin silk] as may their wives and daughters. Men and women of this rank above the age of seventy may wear garments made of coarse silk.

Item: All those of a rank below that of Samurai should use only cotton clothing. They may use coarse pongee for their obi and men and women above the age of seventy will be permitted to wear undergarments of coarse pongee.[66]

Austerity rules usually applied only to vassals of daimyo, while the daimyo themselves and their families lived luxuriously. Much of this spending was required by the shogunate to keep daimyo from becoming too wealthy and powerful. They were required to maintain residences in Edo as well as in their own provinces, and they were expected to entertain lavishly. Traveling back and forth between their provinces and the capital city had to be done in style with many retainers, horses, and equipment. Although they lived in luxury, many daimyo were heavily in debt.

Another source of employment for samurai in peacetime was the central government, or *bakufu*, first established by Shogun Yoritomo in the early thirteenth century. During the period of civil wars, when the *bakufu* was ineffective, daimyo more or less governed their own domains. When Ieyasu came to power, he allowed the daimyo to continue managing local affairs, but reestablished a strong *bakufu* for national matters.

Samurai served as guards and held a wide variety of bureaucratic positions in the *bakufu*.

A young samurai in 1870 poses in his armor. By the time this photo was taken, the samurai class was disappearing as the Meiji rulers abolished the daimyo system and brought their lands under government control.

However, there were still more samurai than positions to be filled so a single job was often held by two or more men on a rotating basis.

The *Ronin* Problem

Probably the most hard-pressed samurai in Tokugawa times were the *ronin*. Although Ieyasu spared the lives of opposing daimyo after the Battle of Sekigahara, he did not spare their fortunes. Collcutt, Jansen, and Kumakura state, "The Bakufu could and did relieve *daimyo* of office, move them at will to other domains, or confiscate all or part of their domains. In the 40 years after 1603, when the Bakufu was established, 71 *daimyo* households were subjected to attainder [confiscation]. . . . Thus one third of the *daimyo* in the country were replaced."[67]

Samurai retainers whose masters were killed in fighting or were ousted later by Ieyasu became *ronin*, masterless samurai, with no means of livelihood. This was not a new problem, as centuries of warfare had created many masterless samurai in the past. However, the upheavals of civil war had created greater numbers of *ronin* in a shorter time than ever before. Writing about the *ronin* situation, historian Catharina Blomberg says:

As a result of the fall of Osaka Castle and the final defeat of the Toyotomi faction [by Ieyasu in 1615] 50,000 *ronin* are esti-

Ronin

Even though samurai became *ronin* through no fault of their own, they were often shabbily treated by samurai in good standing. In this excerpt from *The Fighting Spirit of Japan* by E. J. Harrison (quoted in *Secrets of the Samurai* by Oscar Ratti and Adele Westbrook), three samurai challenged a *ronin* to a duel because the *ronin* had accidentally touched the scabbard of one of the samurai. Judging from his shabby clothes, the *ronin* was obviously very poor, but what followed next showed that poverty had not dulled his skills with a sword.

"In accordance with custom, the combatants exchanged names and swords were unsheathed, the three samurai on one side facing the solitary opponent with whom the sympathies of the onlookers obviously lay. The keen blades of the duellists glittered in the sun. The ronin, as calm as though engaged merely in a friendly fencing bout, ad-

vanced steadily with the point of his weapon directed against the samurai in the centre of the trio, and apparently indifferent to an attack on either flank. The samurai in the middle gave ground inch by inch and the ronin as surely stepped forward. Then the right-hand samurai, who thought he saw an opening, rushed to the attack, but the ronin, who had clearly anticipated this move, parried and with lightning rapidity cut his enemy down with a mortal blow. The left-hand samurai came on in his turn but was treated in similar fashion, a single stroke felling him to the ground bathed in blood. All this took almost less time than it takes to tell. The samurai in the centre, seeing the fate of his comrades, thought better of his first intention and took to his heels."

The *ronin* then went to the local magistrate's office and reported what had happened as required by law.

mated to have roamed about the country in search of reemployment, or, since the chances of finding a new lord were slight indeed, any form of livelihood. Those who possessed sufficient learning might become teachers of Confucianism, *jusha* [Confucian scholars], or instructors in the art of swordsmanship, and there was also the possibility of taking the tonsure [shaving the head] and entering a Zen Buddhist monastery or some other school of Buddhism. Other *ronin*, however, became outlaws or joined the criminal underworld of the major cities.[68]

It was in Tokugawa times that the revenge of the forty-seven *ronin* took place, dramatizing the plight of honorable samurai who, through no fault of their own, were exiled from the system.

The Pleasures of Peacetime

Political history unaccompanied by social and cultural studies often obscures the fact that human beings find pleasure and manage to be creative even in the worst of times. In spite of financial problems and other hardships endured by samurai in Tokugawa times, there were enormous compensations, not the least of which was a cessation of fighting. Historian Harold Bolitho sums up the positive aspects of the Tokugawa period:

> In many important respects, indeed, the centuries of Tokugawa rule provided the *han* [domains] with far more security than they had ever known. To begin with, the Tokugawa peace had freed them from their major Sengoku [civil war] fear: each other . . . under the Tokugawa bakufu, if the *han* were restrained as never before,

they were also protected. For more than 250 years no *han* took up arms against another. There were disputes among them, of course, but these went to the bakufu for arbitration, and even the smallest *han* could expect protection.[69]

Nevertheless, peacetime was still a difficult adjustment for men thoroughly trained in the art of war. Fortunately, many samurai had other talents and skills on which to rely. Even in their glory days as warriors, samurai had always supplemented the martial arts with literary studies. Some of the most hardened military leaders advocated learning and were themselves devoted to artistic pastimes—Yoritomo to poetry, Hideyoshi to the tea ceremony, and Ieyasu to No drama.

With knowledge in fields other than war, many middle- and upper-class samurai entered the Tokugawa period already equipped for peacetime professions. One of the most prominent playwrights of Tokugawa times was Chikamatsu Monzaemon, an unemployed samurai from the lower ranks who found a new profession writing dramas for the Kabuki theater. Matsuo Basho was a samurai who became a Buddhist priest and one of Japan's most honored poets.

Hundreds of other not-so-well-known samurai took up a variety of peacetime occupations. In *Women of the Mito Domain*, Yamakawa Kikue tells of the school operated by her grandfather for children of samurai, merchants, and farmers. He was also a historian and writer who compiled a history of Japan. Nor were these isolated cases according to Collcutt, Jansen, and Kumakura. They write:

> It was the samurai who became the leading intellectuals of the age, the students of Confucianism, Dutch studies, and later of national defense and Western studies.

A woodcut of a Kabuki actor. Because they had training in the arts, many samurai made a smooth transition to peacetime occupations. Some, like Chikamatsu Monzaemon, used their literary talents to become playwrights for Kabuki and No theater.

For the performance of their official administrative duties literacy and basic numeracy [arithmetic] became essential for all samurai. By the late 18th century most domains had opened schools where they employed Confucian scholars and experts in martial arts or Western studies to educate young samurai. A few domains also supported schools for the children of farmers and merchants. Thus the Edo period saw the transformation of samurai from warriors into administrators.[70]

Unfortunately, samurai of the lower ranks were not always so well equipped or so well favored, and it was their disenchantment that eventually helped bring the Tokugawa era to a tumultuous close.

Troubles in the *Bakufu*

Over centuries of samurai rule, Japan's population had grown larger and become urbanized. However, the country's economic basis was still agriculture, and although there had been many improvements in farming, it became more and more difficult to support the growing population on an agriculture base. An added burden was the large-scale spending of the ruling classes (shogunate, daimyo, and imperial court) who consumed so much of the country's resources for their own pleasures and interests.

Some of the shoguns who ruled during Tokugawa times tried to cut back on waste and extravagance, but others only added to it. One shogun who ruled for fifty years had forty wives and concubines in his households. Others spent enormous sums building temples and shrines. Eventually, the *bakufu* had to borrow (or simply take) from the domains, who in turn increased taxes on farmers and reduced samurai stipends.

Living on meager, fixed incomes, lower-class samurai began to see themselves as victims rather than privileged persons. The despised merchants and even some of the lowly peasants were living a lot better than poorer samurai, and the lives of these peasants were not hemmed in with so many social restrictions.

Moreover, samurai felt cheated by their lords who "borrowed" rice allotments from them, reducing their stipends, while they, the lords, continued to live well. Hane remarks, "This practice [of reducing stipends] . . . forced the samurai to fall deeper and deeper into debt, and had the effect of weakening the samurai's sense of loyalty to their lords, who, they felt, were failing in their duty to provide them with adequate means of living."[71]

In the meantime, many daimyo, too, were financially strapped. In order to keep up appearances, they had to swallow their pride and borrow from the wealthy merchants they despised. Sometimes the *bakufu* came to their rescue by forcing merchants to settle for

less than full repayment of loans or even to cancel debts owed by daimyo. However, it only helped for a while until the whole cycle of overspending repeated itself.

By the late eighteenth and early nineteenth centuries, the net effect of all these problems was a growing dissatisfaction with the shogunate and samurai dominance. Into this uneasy state of affairs came an unexpected and unwelcome visitor—Commodore Matthew C. Perry of the U.S. Navy. On July 8, 1853, Perry sailed into Edo Bay in command of four warships.

Commodore Perry's Visit

Perry's mission, authorized by President Millard Fillmore, was to secure permission for

Commodore Matthew Perry steamed American warships into Japanese waters in order to secure permission to trade with the previously isolated nation.

President Fillmore's Letter to the Emperor of Japan

A letter to the emperor of Japan from President Millard Fillmore was delivered with great pomp and ceremony to the emperor's delegation (not the emperor himself) by U.S. Navy Commodore Matthew C. Perry on July 14, 1853. Below are passages from Fillmore's letter excerpted from *Commodore Perry in the Land of the Shogun* by Rhoda Blumberg.

"Great and Good Friend:

I send you this public letter by Commodore Matthew C. Perry, an officer of highest rank in the Navy of the United States, and commander of the squadron now visiting Your Imperial Majesty's domain.

I have directed Commodore Perry to assure your Imperial Majesty that I entertain the kindest feelings toward your Majesty's person and government, and that I have no other object in sending him to Japan but to propose to your Imperial Majesty that the United States and Japan should live in friendship and have commercial intercourse with each other. . . .

We know that the ancient laws of your Imperial Majesty's government do not allow of foreign trade except with the Dutch. But as the state of the world changes, and new governments are formed, it seems to be wise from time to time to make new laws. . . . If Your Imperial Majesty is not satisfied that it would be safe, altogether, to abrogate [abolish] the ancient laws which forbid trade, they might be suspended for five or ten years, so as to try the experiment. . . .

Commodore Perry is also directed by me to represent to your Imperial Majesty that we understand there is a great abundance of coal and provisions in the empire of Japan. . . . We wish that our steamships and other vessels should be allowed to stop in Japan and supply themselves with coal, provisions, and water. They will pay for them in money, or anything else Your Imperial Majesty's subjects may prefer. . . .

These are the only objects for which I have sent Commodore Perry with a powerful squadron to pay a visit to Your Imperial Majesty's renowned city of Edo: friendship, commerce, a supply of coal, and provisions and protection for our shipwrecked people. . . .

May the Almighty have Your Imperial Majesty in his great and holy keeping! In witness whereof I have caused the great seal of the United States to be hereunto affixed, and have subscribed the same with my name, at the city of Washington in America, the seal of my government, on the thirteenth day of the month of November, in the year one thousand eight hundred and fifty two.

Your good friend,
Millard Fillmore"

American ships to stop in Japanese ports for refueling and supplies, to demand humane treatment for shipwrecked American seamen, and to establish a trading relationship with Japan. Perry was not the first to try to break Japan's isolation. The Russians, Dutch, and English had all made previous attempts and the United States had tried once before, but Perry's was the first mission that refused to be turned away.

Ignoring the frantic signals from small Japanese boats to turn back, Perry sailed into the harbor and refused to leave until he had presented President Fillmore's message to the appropriate persons. After delivering his message, Perry sailed away, promising to return in a few months for an answer.

The coming of the "black ships" (as the Japanese called Perry's warships) literally threw the country into panic. The ruling shogun, an indecisive leader, turned to his high officials and the daimyo for advice. Some of the more militant samurai were outraged at the intruders and wanted to resist at all costs. To others, equally outraged but more realistic, it was obvious that Japanese technology was no match for that of the "red barbarians," as people from Western nations were called.

The best policy, according to these advisers, was to open Japan's doors to learn everything possible about Western technology. By so doing, Japan would be able to hold its own among world powers. They further argued that opening up the country did not mean giving up sacred national traditions as many feared.

At length, a decision was made to sign a treaty with Commodore Perry allowing American ships to enter Japanese ports for supplies. (Actual trade agreements were worked out at a later date.) Before Perry returned, however, *bakufu* officials thought the decision might be more readily accepted if they got the approval of the emperor, who was not usually consulted in political matters. Emissaries were sent to the emperor fully expecting to obtain his blessings, but to their surprise, he refused.

Once Japan opened its doors to foreigners, Americans and Europeans became common sights in Japanese ports. Instead of trying to rid the nation of the "red barbarians," the Japanese decided to seize the opportunity to learn about Western technology.

Since his approval was just a formality anyway and the decision was already made, the *bakufu* had to go ahead as planned.

When Perry returned in February of the following year, a treaty was signed despite the emperor's objections. This action provided an occasion for groups of young militant samurai to rally behind the emperor. Known as *shishi,* "men of high purpose," they were mostly lower-class samurai who were expert in the martial arts and who used terrorist tactics to further their cause. Their battle cry was "Re-vere the Emperor and expel the barbarians." Hane says of the *shishi:*

> These samurai . . . were inclined to be fiery extremists as well as fanatical political activists. They were usually expert swordsmen who rigorously upheld such traditional samurai values as duty, courage, and honor. Some of the shishi outgrew their earlier limitations and managed to emerge as perspicacious [wise] statesmen; by and large, however, they were

The Coming of the "Black Ships"

In the following excerpt from *A Daughter of the Samurai,* Etsu Inagaki Sugimoto retells the story her grandmother told her about the 1853 visit to Edo harbor of Commodore Perry and his four warships, which the Japanese called the "black ships."

"'Honourable Grandmother,' she [Sugimoto] said, pointing to a coloured map of the world, 'I am much, much troubled. I have just learned that our beloved land is only a few tiny islands in the great world.'

The grandmother adjusted her big horn spectacles and for a few minutes carefully studied the map. Then with slow dignity she closed the book. 'It is quite natural, little Etsu-bo, for them to make Japan look small on this map,' she said. 'It was made by the people of the black ships. Japan is made large on the Japanese maps of the world.'

'Who are the people of the black ships?' asked the little girl.

'They are the red barbarians who came uninvited to our sacred land. They came in big black ships that moved without sails.'

'. . . I wonder why they were called "black ships." Do you know, Honourable Grandmother?'

'Because far out on the waters they looked like clouds of black smoke rolling nearer and nearer, and they had long black guns that roared. The red barbarians cared nothing for beauty.'

'. . . And after that?' asked the eager little voice. 'And after that, honourable Grandmother?'

'The black ships and the rude barbarians sailed away,' she concluded, with a deep sigh. 'But they sailed back many times. They are always sailing. And now the people of our sacred land also talk like tradesmen and no longer are peaceful and content.'

'Will they never be peaceful and content again?' asked the little girl with anxious eyes. 'The honourable teacher said that sailing ships bring lands nearer to each other.'

'Listen!' said the grandmother, holding herself very straight. 'Little Granddaughter, unless the red barbarians and the children of the gods learn each other's hearts, the ships may sail and sail, but the two lands will never be nearer.'"

Disgruntled samurai who wanted to expel all foreigners from Japan brought down the bakufu *government and restored power to the emperor. Their dream of returning to the old ways, however, did not last long.*

men who lacked the vision to discern a meaningful role and place for Japan in the context of the changing world scene. . . . They were convinced that they were on the side of truth, justice, and right, and that they were the only true patriots while those who failed to agree with them were self-serving traitors.[72]

Beset with pressure from foreigners, disgruntled daimyo, a disapproving emperor, and *shishi* activists, the *bakufu* was overwhelmed.

Once more civil strife erupted in Japan. Fortunately, this time it did not last as long nor was it as widespread as in the days of warring daimyo.

Nevertheless, it brought an end to the Tokugawa era. In 1867, fourteen years after Commodore Perry steamed into Edo harbor, the *bakufu* fell and the emperor was restored to power. Although the samurai who helped bring down the *bakufu* probably did not recognize it yet, this was also the beginning of the end for the samurai.

End of the Samurai

It may seem odd that samurai would help bring about their own destruction, but, as Robert Bellah explains in a study of the Tokugawa period, "It is important then to realize what was their social position under the old regime. . . . They had a legitimized status as rulers [in regard to] the common people but they had very little else which committed them in any rigid sense to the old system. They had no land and not even adequate stipends."[73]

On the other hand, they had a lot to gain by the overthrow for it was many lower-ranked samurai who became leaders in the new government. Bellah continues, "It was largely from their ranks that the new . . . government was formed and they provided the leadership for many of the innovations, economic and cultural as well as governmental, of the new era."[74]

In 1867, the new samurai leaders succeeded in persuading Keiki, the ruling shogun, to return his commission to the emperor as a prelude to establishing some form of parliamentary government. Feeling this was the best solution to the serious problems facing the country, Keiki complied, returning power to the emperor for the first time in hundreds of years.

Although he was undoubtedly sincere about wanting the best for his country, Keiki also believed he would be rewarded with a high office in the new government. In this matter, he was gravely mistaken. Daimyo who wanted an end to the Tokugawa *bakufu* op-posed any role for him whatsoever. To this end, they provoked him and his followers into an armed conflict. Keiki's forces were defeated and he was stripped of his lands and forced into retirement.

After the power shift, victorious leaders began forming a new government called the Meiji Restoration. The central figure of the new regime was fifteen-year-old Emperor Mutsuhito, later known as Emperor Meiji. The imperial capital was moved from Kyoto to Edo, or Tokyo as it is called today. Restoring the emperor caused no problems with the general public because the emperor had always been held in high esteem from ancient times forward.

Actually, the real power still lay behind the throne with the reformers. The young emperor was barely aware of the political currents swirling around him, but he made hundreds of public appearances so the people would get to know him and accept him as head of the government. Protected by the awesomeness of the imperial court, the restoration leaders began working out a completely new direction for Japan.

Samurai Under Meiji Rule

What the Meiji Restoration meant for the samurai was not just an end to their dominance as the ruling class, but the end of the samurai class altogether. This fall from grace did not happen abruptly but was years in the making. First, the vast landholdings of the daimyo were brought under the control of the central government, a move welcomed by most daimyo as a way out of their financial troubles. In 1871, domains were abolished completely and replaced with larger political units called prefectures. Daimyo, under different titles, continued to be influential within the new regime.

With the domains abolished, the new central government had to accept responsibility for paying thousands of samurai stipends formerly paid by daimyo. This burden soon proved too great a drain on the national treasury, and various efforts to reduce the load were made. Eventually, samurai stipends were

Mutsuhito, the Emperor Meiji, was fifteen when he assumed the throne. He had little political experience and was content to let his advisers direct the progress of the Meiji Restoration.

converted into interest-bearing bonds based on the value of the stipends and given as a onetime payment.

As usual, this action favored high-ranking samurai far more than those in the low statuses. Historian W. G. Beasley comments, "For the more affluent samurai and their feudal lords, it provided useful capital sums in treasury bonds, which could be used to finance investment in land or some forms of modern enterprise. For the poorest, it completed the process of impoverishment that had been going on for generations, forcing them back to the land or into other kinds of productive employment."[75]

Losing their stipends was only the beginning. Within the next few years, the old class structure was dismantled and with it the privileged status of the samurai. They were forbidden to wear the special hairstyle and distinctive clothing that set them apart from other classes. The crowning blow came in 1876 when an edict was issued banning the wearing of swords for everyone except members of the new conscript army.

The decision to establish a conscript (draft) army largely made up of commoners instead of samurai was based on several factors. One was the belief that samurai would not be able to put aside old rivalries from clan warfare days to form a cohesive national unit. Another was that peasant soldiers were easier to train and not as reluctant as samurai to use new weapons such as guns and cannon. And so, with the establishment of a conscript army, even the time-honored profession of warrior was taken from them.

Samurai Reaction

Samurai reaction to the restoration depended upon their social ranking and personal circumstances. For some it brought relief. Daimyo and upper-class samurai saw it as a way to escape their financial burdens but still retain power, wealth, and influence. Samurai in the lower ranks who had long since given up the old ideals now enjoyed freedom from dozens of pointless social restrictions imposed upon them. This freedom from social constraints was also a relief for many samurai in the upper ranks.

On the other hand, some lower-class members were dismayed at the reforms, especially former samurai who had lost their masters but had been still allowed to act as samurai in some of the domains. Called *goshi*, they held positions in local government such as policemen and village headmen until the Meiji period. Historian Stephen Vlastos says of them:

> Goshi headmen governed hamlets of up to twenty households and lorded over the peasants like the estate managers of the medieval period. . . . Meiji reforms struck at the very heart of *goshi* privilege. Like castle town samurai, they were accustomed to thinking of themselves as an elite, superior in status, if not always in wealth, to commoners. And as the lowest-ranking status group within the warrior

Late nineteenth-century samurai lost most of the former trappings that indicated their rank. Only the swords in this 1868 photograph reveal the warrior status of these samurai.

A group of policemen march off to quell the rebellion in Satsuma. The revolt lasted seven months, but the forces of the Meiji government brought an end to the last efforts of samurai resistance.

class, they perhaps felt even more keenly the loss of the symbols of elite status, such as the right to bear arms.[76]

The Last Rebellion

It was samurai such as the *goshi* who eagerly participated in the last serious resistance to the Meiji Restoration, the Satsuma Rebellion of 1877. Daimyo who were instrumental in bringing about the restoration expected to dominate the new government. However, when policies went contrary to their wishes, some of them staged uprisings, which were quickly put down by government troops.

One of these rebellions, however, turned into a full-scale revolt. It was led by Saigo Takamori, a prominent daimyo from the Satsuma domain. Takamori had been a major force in bringing about the restoration, but later, when he became disillusioned with some of its policies, he resigned and returned to his former domain where he was now governor. When he did so, a lot of his followers, including many military men, accompanied him. Whether Takamori intended to stage a rebellion from the beginning or whether the idea just grew as his cadre of loyal followers grew is unknown, but preparations for war in the old Satsuma domain rapidly escalated.

In February 1877, Takamori with a well-trained army of samurai and commoners marched against the capital and a full-scale war began. It was the severest test the new government and the conscript army had faced so far, and victory was not easily won. The fighting continued for seven months with great loss of life on both sides. Vlastos says:

> To defeat the large and well-trained rebel forces, the government had to mobilize the entire standing army and reserves and enlist an additional 7,000 *shizoku* [middle-rank samurai] as "police" auxiliaries. Of the 65,000 soldiers sent to the front, 6,000 were killed in action, and 10,000 were wounded. The financial cost of prosecuting the war was staggering. Direct expenditures totaled 42 million [yen], a sum equal to 80 percent of the annual budget.[77]

The Satsuma Rebellion was the last hurrah for the samurai. It had all the legendary heroics of medieval days, including stories of samurai women fighting off government troops with spears. When his forces were finally routed, Saigo Takamori took his own life on the battlefield. Branded as a rebel in his own time, today he is revered as a noble samurai who fought and died for what he deemed was honorable and right.

After quashing the Satsuma Rebellion, the restoration government continued its policy of reforms intended to make Japan a competitor in international affairs. Most samurai did as they had done before—adapted to new conditions and entered new occupations. Others clung to a vanished past, not quite understanding what had happened to their lives. Writer Etsu Sugimoto's family was among those who resisted the restoration forces. "When my mother learned that her husband's cause was lost and he taken prisoner," Sugimoto writes, "she sent her household to a place of safety, and then, to prevent the mansion from falling into the hands of the enemy, she with her own hands set fire to it and from the mountain-side watched it burn to the ground."[78]

Sugimoto's father was later released and returned home where he was required, as a high-ranking samurai, to serve as governor until the restoration government could take over. On his return, he had a modest home built for his family on the ashes of the former mansion and tried to pick up the pieces of his life. Sugimoto says of her father:

> He planted a mulberry grove on a few acres of land near by and prided himself on having levelled his rank to the class of farmer. Men of samurai rank knew nothing about business. It had always been considered a disgrace for them to handle money; so the management of all business affairs was left to faithful but wholly inexperienced Jiya [a family retainer], while Father devoted his life to reading, to memories, and to introducing unwelcome ideas of progressive reform to his less advanced neighbors.[79]

The Enduring Samurai Spirit

In the long run, what survived after the dissolution of the samurai class were those principles accentuated in the code of Bushido—duty, devotion, and courage, combined with a taste for artistic pursuits.

Enjoyment of artistic pursuits still may be seen in the popularity of the tea ceremony, flower arranging, calligraphy, gardening, and traditional Japanese poetry in many Western countries as well as in Japan. All of these specialties were enjoyed by generations of samurai and brought to heights of perfection under their patronage.

Another surviving aspect of warrior training is evident today in the prominence of the martial arts, not only in Japan but worldwide. In addition, many observers contend that the

Part of the samurai spirit remains in many of the martial arts now practiced all over the world. Training, dedication, and fortitude are hallmarks of these popular sports.

samurai spirit lives on in Japanese business practices wherein loyalty and devotion to one's company is akin to loyalty to one's lord.

Undoubtedly, the most dramatic and tragic legacy from the samurai warrior code was the duty of self-sacrifice carried out in World War II by kamikaze pilots who deliberately crashed their warplanes into U.S. battleships. (The pilots were named for the miraculous winds that destroyed Mongol invaders in the thirteenth century.) Moreover, when defeated, hundreds of Japanese soldiers killed themselves on Pacific Island battlefields rather than surrender.

This intense samurai spirit of duty and selflessness is eloquently expressed in a poem written in the thirteenth century by Shogun Minamoto Sanetomo, an accomplished poet whose own life was cut short by an assassin.

Though a time come
when mountains crack
and seas go dry,
never to my lord
will I be found double-hearted! [80]

Notes

Introduction: The Emergence of the Samurai

1. Jonathan Norton Leonard, *Early Japan.* New York: Time-Life Books, 1968, p. 56.
2. Mikiso Hane, *Premodern Japan: A Historical Survey.* Boulder, CO: Westview Press, 1991, p. 71.

Chapter 1: Professional Warriors

3. Oscar Ratti and Adele Westbrook, *Secrets of the Samurai: The Martial Arts of Feudal Japan.* Rutland, VT: Charles E. Tuttle, 1973, p. 230.
4. Stephen R. Turnbull, *The Book of the Samurai: The Warrior Class of Japan.* New York: Arco Publishing, 1982, p. 28.
5. Leonard, *Early Japan,* p. 68.
6. Quoted in Turnbull, *The Book of the Samurai,* p. 24.
7. John Newman, *Bushido: The Way of the Warrior: A New Perspective on the Japanese Military Tradition.* New York: Gallery Books, 1989, p. 24.
8. Leonard, *Early Japan,* p. 77.
9. Quoted in Helen Craig McCullough, trans., *Genji & Heike: Selections from* The Tale of Genji *and* The Tale of the Heike. Stanford, CA: Stanford University Press, 1994, p. 425.
10. Stephen Turnbull, *Samurai: The Warrior Tradition.* London: Arms and Armour Press, 1996, p. 289.
11. Fred Neff, *Lessons from the Samurai.* Minneapolis: Lerner Publications, 1987, p. 12.
12. Leonard, *Early Japan,* p. 78.
13. Turnbull, *The Book of the Samurai,* p. 66.
14. Turnbull, *The Book of the Samurai,* p. 66.
15. Newman, *Bushido: The Way of the Warrior,* p. 90.
16. Stephen Turnbull, *Battles of the Samurai.* London: Arms and Armour Press, 1987, p. 19.
17. H. Paul Varley, *Japanese Culture: A Short History.* Tokyo: Charles E. Tuttle, 1973, p. 75.

Chapter 2: Becoming a Samurai Warrior

18. Neff, *Lessons from the Samurai,* p. 12.
19. Neff, *Lessons from the Samurai,* p. 12.
20. Newman, *Bushido: The Way of the Warrior,* p. 72.
21. Catharina Blomberg, *The Heart of the Warrior: Origins and Religious Background of the Samurai in Feudal Japan.* Sandgate, Folkstone, Kent: Japan Library, 1994, p. 69.
22. Leonard, *Early Japan,* p. 72.
23. Quoted in Miyamoto Musashi, *The Book of Five Rings* (including *The Book of Family Traditions on the Art of War* by Yagyu Munenori), ed. and trans. Thomas Cleary. Boston: Shambhala, 1993, pp. 81, 108.
24. Winston L. King, *Zen and the Way of the Sword: Arming the Samurai Psyche.* Oxford: Oxford University Press, 1993, p. 63.
25. Quoted in Musashi, *The Book of Five Rings,* p. 69.
26. Quoted in Musashi, *The Book of Five Rings,* p. 65.
27. Martin Collcutt, Marius Jansen, and Isao Kumakura, *Cultural Atlas of Japan.* New York: Facts On File, 1988, pp. 107–108.
28. Collcutt, Jansen, and Kumakura, *Cultural Atlas of Japan,* p. 118.

29. Musashi, *The Book of Five Rings,* p. 13.
30. Peter Spry-Leverton and Peter Kornicki, *Japan.* New York: Facts On File, 1987, p. 66.
31. Leonard, *Early Japan,* p. 167.
32. Spry-Leverton and Kornicki, *Japan,* pp. 67–68.

Chapter 3: The Code of Bushido

33. King, *Zen and the Way of the Sword,* p. 124.
34. Quoted in William Scott Wilson, trans., *Ideals of the Samurai: Writings of Japanese Warriors.* Burbank, CA: Ohara Publications, 1982, pp. 121–22.
35. Eiko Ikegami, *The Taming of the Samurai: Honorific Individualism and the Making of Modern Japan.* Cambridge, MA: Harvard University Press, 1995, p. 231.
36. Ikegami, *The Taming of the Samurai,* p. 200.
37. King, *Zen and the Way of the Sword,* p. 149.
38. King, *Zen and the Way of the Sword,* p. 153.
39. Blomberg, *The Heart of the Warrior,* p. 79.
40. Quoted in Wilson, *Ideals of the Samurai,* p. 122.
41. Quoted in Newman, *Bushido: The Way of the Warrior,* p. 157.
42. Quoted in Newman, *Bushido: The Way of the Warrior,* pp. 133–36.
43. Blomberg, *The Heart of the Warrior,* p. 176.

Chapter 4: The Changing Nature of Combat

44. Yoshiaki Shimizu, ed., *Japan: The Shaping of Daimyo Culture 1185–1868.* New York: George Braziller, 1988, p. 26.
45. Turnbull, *Samurai: The Warrior Tradition,* pp. 233–34.

46. Asao Naohiro, "The Sixteenth Century Unification," in *The Cambridge History of Japan: Early Modern Japan,* vol. 4, ed. John Whitney Hall. Cambridge: Cambridge University Press, 1991, p. 54.
47. Henry Wiencek, *The Lords of Japan.* Chicago: Stonehenge Press, 1982, p. 122.
48. Naohiro, "The Sixteenth Century Unification," p. 49.
49. Wiencek, *The Lords of Japan,* p. 113.
50. Wiencek, *The Lords of Japan,* p. 124.
51. John Whitney Hall, "The *Bakuhan* System," in *The Cambridge History of Japan,* vol. 4, p. 144.

Chapter 5: Samurai at Home

52. Quoted in Katsu Kokichi, *Musui's Story: The Autobiography of a Tokugawa Samurai,* trans. and ed. Teruko Craig. Tucson: University of Arizona Press, 1988, p. xiv.
53. Hane, *Premodern Japan,* p. 71.
54. Yamakawa Kikue, *Women of the Mito Domain: Recollections of Samurai Family Life.* Tokyo: University of Tokyo Press, 1992, p. 103.
55. Quoted in Ivan Morris, trans. and ed., *The Pillow Book of Sei Shonagon.* Baltimore: Penguin Books, 1971, p. 39.
56. Kikue, *Women of the Mito Domain,* p. 109.
57. Quoted in Kikue, *Women of the Mito Domain,* p. 172.
58. Susan B. Hanley, "Tokugawa Society: Material Culture, Standard of Living, and Life Styles," in *The Cambridge History of Japan,* vol. 4, p. 666.
59. Hane, *Premodern Japan,* p. 154.
60. Kikue, *Women of the Mito Domain,* pp. 41–42.
61. Wiencek, *The Lords of Japan,* p. 87.
62. Collcutt, Jansen, and Kumakura, *Cultural Atlas of Japan,* p. 154.

63. Kikue, *Women of the Mito Domain*, pp. 79–80.

Chapter 6: Samurai in Peacetime

64. Hane, *Premodern Japan*, p. 143.
65. Collcutt, Jansen, and Kumakura, *Cultural Atlas of Japan*, p. 144.
66. Quoted in Kikue, *Women of the Mito Domain*, p. 40.
67. Collcutt, Jansen, and Kumakura, *Cultural Atlas of Japan*, p. 134.
68. Blomberg, *The Heart of the Warrior*, p. 154.
69. Harold Bolitho, "The *Han*," in *The Cambridge History of Japan*, vol. 4., p. 202.
70. Collcutt, Jansen, and Kumakura, *Cultural Atlas of Japan*, p. 146.
71. Hane, *Premodern Japan*, p. 193.
72. Hane, *Premodern Japan*, p. 215.

Epilogue: End of the Samurai

73. Robert Bellah, *Tokugawa Religion: The Cultural Roots of Japan*. New York: Free Press, 1957, p. 45.
74. Bellah, *Tokugawa Religion*, p. 45.
75. W. G. Beasley, "Meiji Political Institutions," in *The Cambridge History of Japan: The Nineteenth Century*, vol. 5, ed. Marius B. Jansen. Cambridge: Cambridge University Press, 1989, p. 640.
76. Stephen Vlastos, "Opposition Movements in Early Meiji, 1868–1885," in *The Cambridge History of Japan*, vol. 5, p. 395.
77. Vlastos, "Opposition Movements in Early Meiji, 1868–1885," p. 398.
78. Etsu Inagaki Sugimoto, *A Daughter of the Samurai*. Garden City, NY: Doubleday, Doran, 1930, p. 5.
79. Sugimoto, *A Daughter of the Samurai*, p. 5.
80. Quoted in Hiroaki Sato and Burton Watson, eds., *From the Country of Eight Islands*. Seattle: University of Washington Press, 1981, p. 223.

Glossary

ashigaru: Foot soldiers below the rank of samurai.

Ashikaga: A samurai clan who came to power in the fourteenth century.

bakufu: Central government set up by Minamoto Yoritomo when he became the first permanent shogun in 1185. Its literal meaning is "tent government."

black ships: Term used by the Japanese to designate Commodore Perry's fleet of steam-powered warships.

bu: Japanese word referring to martial arts.

bun: Japanese word referring to literary arts.

bushi: Japanese warrior; (*bu*) war, (*shi*) man.

Bushido: Ethical code of the warrior; (*bushi*) warrior, (*do*) way; literally, "way of the warrior."

calligraphy: Fine handwriting done with ink and brush.

concubine: Women (other than wives) who lived in wealthy samurai households and bore children by the head of the household to assure a male heir.

daimyo: Wealthy warlords who governed large estates called domains, or *han*, and employed many samurai retainers, warriors, managers, and workers.

do-maru: Simple wraparound armor worn by low-status samurai; made of thin metal plates (lamellae) that were laced together.

Edo: Name of the village that eventually became the city of Tokyo.

feudal system: An economic and political arrangement whereby strong leaders (lords) provided jobs and protection for their followers (vassals) in return for the vassals' services and loyal support.

genbuku: Coming-of-age ceremony for a samurai boy at the age of fifteen or sixteen.

geta: Wooden clogs worn with special socks (see *tabi*) and held on the feet by thongs.

go: A popular board game resembling chess.

goshi: Masterless samurai who were allowed to hold minor offices in some domains.

Hagakure: A militant version of the code of Bushido compiled in the seventeenth century by Yamamoto Tsunetomo.

hakama: Wide-legged trousers worn over a robe by samurai men.

han: A term referring to the domain of a daimyo and to the system of local government within it.

haori: A short, blouselike jacket often worn with *hakama*.

hara-kiri: A slang name for ritual suicide; literally means "to cut the belly."

harquebus: An early type of firearm introduced into Japan by the Portuguese in the seventeenth century.

Heian: The courtly period in Japanese history preceding the samurai era; famous for great achievements in art and literature.

Kabuki theater: Popular entertainment for townspeople in the Tokugawa period. *Bakufu* leaders tried to curb its popularity and discourage samurai from attending, but without much success.

kamikaze pilots: Japanese fighter pilots in World War II who flew suicide missions against U.S. battleships. They took their name from the great wind that saved Japan from the Mongol army invasions of the thirteenth century.

kamishimo: A samurai man's formal dress outfit consisting of a sleeveless jacket with wide, stiffened shoulders worn with an underrobe and *hakama.*

katana: The curved, long sword carried by a samurai outside the home. In the Tokugawa period, it was considered to be "the soul of a samurai" and only samurai were legally allowed to own and wear it.

kenka: Personal quarrels and vendetta among samurai.

kimono: Literally means "clothing," but has come to specify outer robes worn by Japanese men and women.

koku: A unit of measurement meaning the amount of rice to sustain a man for one year. Samurai stipends were paid in *koku,* either the rice itself or equivalent currency.

lamellar armor: Light but effective Japanese armor made of thin metal plates laced together with colorful cords.

Meiji: Literally meaning "enlightened rule," it was the name given to both the movement that restored the emperor to power in the nineteenth century and the emperor himself. Emperor Mutsuhito became Emperor Meiji.

mons: Family crests displayed on flags and uniforms.

naginata: A weapon consisting of a curved blade attached to a long pole, often used by samurai women.

No theater: A type of drama on a bare stage enjoyed by elite samurai. It combined music, drama, dancing, elaborate costumes, and masks.

obi: Sash tied around the waist of a woman's kimono.

Pure Land Buddhism: A type of Buddhism that taught that all believers could find blissful rest, not just the few who spent their lives seeking enlightenment. It became very popular with samurai.

ronin: Samurai warriors who were left masterless at the death or disgrace of their lords, thereby losing the privileges of their class.

samurai: A name for a special class of Japanese warriors that first came into use in the twelfth century. It literally meant "one who serves." Over the centuries, it came to signify an entire class of warriors and military leaders divided into many subclasses.

sashimono: A clan flag on a pole attached to the back of a warrior's armor that was useful in identifying troops in combat. The flags were secured to a horizontal frame at the top of the pole so they would always stay unfurled.

Satsuma Rebellion: An uprising of dissident samurai and commoners after the Meiji Restoration. It was led by Saigo Takamori and was put down with great difficulty by the new government's conscript army.

Sekigahara: The name of the village where a decisive battle was fought in the year 1600 in which Tokugawa Ieyasu narrowly defeated the armies of his enemies and completed the unification of Japan.

Sengoku: Name given to the period of civil wars that ravaged the country in the late fifteenth century.

seppuku: Ritual suicide in which the victim stabs himself in the abdomen with a dagger, after which a swordsman cuts off his head. It was done to prevent being captured by an enemy, to atone for disgrace, to protest an unwise course of action, and later, as a sentence for offenses.

Shinto: Original religious system of Japan, which claims a divine origin for the emperor and stresses reverence for nature and for ancestors. It continues to be a major religious system in Japan today.

shishi: Radical samurai from the lower classes who helped bring about the Meiji Restoration in the nineteenth century.

tabi: Socks with a separate pocket for the big toe; worn with thongs or wooden clogs.

Taira: Powerful samurai clan of the twelfth century who first defeated the Minamoto clan, and then were completely annihilated a few years later when the Minamoto staged a comeback. (Also known as the Heike clan.)

Tales of the Heike: A collection of war tales about the Taira (Heike) clan's downfall. Compiled in the thirteenth century, this is one of the most revered works in Japanese literature.

wakizashi: A short sword worn in the belt of a samurai along with his *katana*.

yoroi: An early type of samurai armor made of thin metal plates (lamellae) laced together with colorful cords. It had a very boxlike appearance when worn.

Zen Buddhism: An austere type of Buddhism that taught self-control and strict mental discipline.

For Further Reading

Monique Avakian, *The Meiji Restoration and the Rise of Modern Japan*. Englewood Cliffs, NJ: Silver Burdett Press, 1991. A colorfully illustrated book for young readers about the Meiji period and the events leading up to it.

Michael Gibson, *The Samurai of Japan*. London: Wayland, 1973. Includes all phases of samurai life, particularly the warfare traditions. Black-and-white illustrations realistically depict armor and weapons.

Erik Christian Haugaard, *The Boy and the Samurai*. Boston: Houghton Mifflin, 1991. A novel for young adults set in the *Sengoku* period of the sixteenth century. Although fiction, it is well researched by the author, who lived in Japan.

————, *The Revenge of the Forty-Seven Ronin*. Boston: Houghton Mifflin, 1995. A fictional account for young adults about the forty-seven *ronin* who avenged the death of their master in seventeenth-century Japan. The story is told through the eyes of a young servant of one of the *ronin*.

Susan Kuklin, *Komodo: Children of Japan*. New York: G. P. Putnam, 1995. A book for young readers featuring photographs of modern Japanese children engaging in customs handed down from samurai days, such as calligraphy and fencing.

Brenda Ralph Lewis, *Growing Up in Samurai Japan*. London: Batsford, 1981. Depicts the everyday lives of Japanese people during the days of samurai rule through text and line drawings. For juvenile readers.

Fiona MacDonald, *Samurai Castle*. New York: Peter Bedrick Books, 1995. A beautifully illustrated book about life in samurai castles and castle towns. Although directed to young readers, its drawings are instructive for all ages.

Carole Manchester, *Tea in the East*. New York: Hearst Books, 1996. Included in this interesting book for young adult and adult readers is a chapter on tea drinking in Japan, with many color photographs of tea houses and the tea ceremony.

Don Nardo, *Traditional Japan*. San Diego: Lucent Books, 1995. Excellent overview of Japanese history from ancient times through the nineteenth century that places the samurai in historical context.

Chuck Norris, *The Secret Power Within: Zen Solutions to Real Problems*. Boston: Little, Brown, 1996. In this personal account of his life, a popular martial arts teacher and TV actor explains the meaning of Zen Buddhism as it shaped the martial arts and influenced his life.

Herbert E. Plutschow, *Introducing Kyoto*. Tokyo: Kodansha International, 1979. Contains beautiful color photographs of Kyoto, the ancient capital of Japan. Featured are tea houses, shrines, homes, and gardens—both modern and historic.

Stephen Turnbull, *Samurai Warfare*. London: Arms and Armour Press, 1997. One of the foremost authorities on samurai culture, Turnbull has written many books on the samurai, particularly on the art of war. This book is enlivened with case studies and anecdotes.

Works Consulted

Robert Bellah, *Tokugawa Religion: The Cultural Roots of Japan*. New York: Free Press, 1957. A study of religious currents that shaped the Tokugawa era, including the expulsion and persecution of Christians.

Catharina Blomberg, *The Heart of the Warrior: Origins and Religious Background of the Samurai in Feudal Japan*. Sandgate, Folkstone, Kent: Japan Library, 1994. Explores samurai culture, including information on warrior training, family life, and the code of Bushido.

Rhoda Blumberg, *Commodore Perry in the Land of the Shogun*. New York: Lothrop, Lee & Shepard Books, 1985. This informative and well-illustrated book for young readers presents the story of Commodore Perry's visits to Japan, which ultimately ended that country's self-imposed isolation.

Martin Collcutt, Marius Jansen, and Isao Kumakura, *Cultural Atlas of Japan*. New York: Facts On File, 1988. A monumental work with detailed information and hundreds of illustrations on Japanese political, social, religious, and cultural history from ancient to modern times.

John Whitney Hall, ed., *The Cambridge History of Japan: Early Modern Japan*. Vol. 4. Cambridge: Cambridge University Press, 1991. One of five volumes of a scholarly series written by authorities on Japanese history; for serious readers who want detailed information.

Mikiso Hane, *Premodern Japan: A Historical Survey*. Boulder, CO: Westview Press, 1991. A very readable book on Japanese history before the Meiji Restoration.

Stephen K. Hayes, *The Ninja and Their Secret Fighting Art*. Rutland, VT: Charles E. Tuttle, 1981. For young adult readers, this book tells the story of the mysterious and deadly ninja assassins of medieval Japan, and describes their weapons and tactics.

Eiko Ikegami, *The Taming of the Samurai: Honorific Individualism and the Making of Modern Japan*. Cambridge, MA: Harvard University Press, 1995. Explains how the samurai were gradually transformed from warriors into bureaucrats.

Marius B. Jansen, ed., *The Cambridge History of Japan: The Nineteenth Century*. Vol. 5. Cambridge: Cambridge University Press, 1989. The last of five volumes of a scholarly work by authorities on Japanese history.

David E. Jones, *Women Warriors*. Washington, DC: Brassey, 1997. Contains stories of fighting women throughout the ages, including a section about female samurai warriors.

Kamo-no-Chomei, *Hojoki: Visions of a Torn World*. Berkeley, CA: Stone Bridge Press, 1996. A twelfth-century Japanese poet eloquently describes the trials and tribulations of life in medieval Japan, including earthquakes, fires, and famines.

Yamakawa Kikue, *Women of the Mito Domain: Recollections of Samurai Family Life*. Tokyo: University of Tokyo Press, 1992. Memoirs of a samurai woman that provides a rare account of the domestic aspects of samurai life in the late Tokugawa period.

Winston L. King, *Zen and the Way of the Sword: Arming the Samurai Psyche*. Oxford: Oxford University Press, 1993. Many personal anecdotes about samurai life make this an absorbing book. Contains good discussions on the case of the forty-seven *ronin*, the practice of Zen, and the custom of seppuku.

Katsu Kokichi, *Musui's Story: The Autobiography of a Tokugawa Samurai*. Trans. and ed. Teruko Craig. Tucson: University of Arizona Press, 1988. The engaging self-told story of a scandalous lower-class samurai; interesting and easy to read.

Jonathan Norton Leonard, *Early Japan*. New York: Time-Life Books, 1968. The author's clear and lively writing style makes this a valuable book for those interested in Japan and the samurai but not wanting exhaustive detail. Many illustrations and drawings enhance the text.

David J. Lu, *Japan: A Documentary History*. Armonk, NY: M. E. Sharpe, 1997. An excellent book for primary sources on Japanese history. The author provides background and editorial comments on the selected documents.

Helen Craig McCullough, trans., *Genji & Heike: Selections from* The Tale of Genji *and* The Tale of the Heike. Stanford, CA: Stanford University Press, 1994. Presents excerpts from two of Japan's most revered literary works of ancient times.

Ivan Morris, trans. and ed., *The Pillow Book of Sei Shonagon*. Baltimore: Penguin Books, 1971. Sei Shonagon was a lady-in-waiting to the empress of Japan during the Heian period, just prior to the beginning of the samurai era. She was also a talented writer and poet who kept a journal of personal observations. Her journals were eventually published under the title *The Pillow Book* (referring to notes written in one's bedroom before retiring). *The Pillow Book* is a rich source of information about Heian court life, manners, and fashions.

Miyamoto Musashi, *The Book of Five Rings* (including *The Book of Family Traditions on the Art of War* by Yagyu Munenori). Ed. and trans. Thomas Cleary. Boston: Shambhala, 1993. The two works in this volume are both classics in the study of the martial arts. Written in the seventeenth century by master swordsmen, they are full of interesting observations on life and death.

Fred Neff, *Lessons from the Samurai*. Minneapolis: Lerner Publications, 1987. A short, basic book for young adults on the martial arts, their origin, and philosophical underpinnings.

John Newman, *Bushido: The Way of the Warrior: A New Perspective on the Japanese Military Tradition*. New York: Gallery Books, 1989. Presents the origins of the code of Bushido along with later influences that affected it, such as Confucianism and militarism.

Oscar Ratti and Adele Westbrook, *Secrets of the Samurai: The Martial Arts of Feudal Japan*. Rutland, VT: Charles E. Tuttle, 1973. Contains a wealth of information, not only about the martial arts but about the samurai as well.

Hiroaki Sato and Burton Watson, eds., *From the Country of Eight Islands*. Seattle: University of Washington Press, 1981. A collection of Japanese poems including works of famous samurai poets.

Yoshiaki Shimizu, ed., *Japan: The Shaping of Daimyo Culture 1185–1868*. New York: George Braziller, 1988. The text is beautifully illustrated with full-color photographs of Japanese art treasures associated with daimyo warlords. Included are sections on statuary, painting, sword making, ceramics, and clothing.

Peter Spry-Leverton and Peter Kornicki, *Japan*. New York: Facts On File, 1987. A book of general interest on Japanese culture, past and present; contains many color photographs.

Etsu Inagaki Sugimoto, *A Daughter of the Samurai*. Garden City, NY: Doubleday, Doran, 1930. The author grew up in a well-to-do samurai family in early Meiji times, and later migrated to America where she wrote her recollections of life in Japan. Very readable and entertaining.

Stephen R. Turnbull, *The Book of the Samurai: The Warrior Class of Japan*. New York: Arco Publishing, 1982. This comprehensive volume by one of the leading authorities on samurai history and culture describes all aspects of samurai life throughout the centuries.

———*Battles of the Samurai*. London: Arms and Armour Press, 1987. A few selected battles of major significance are described, along with what each battle site looks like today and how to get there.

———*Samurai: The Warrior Tradition*. London: Arms and Armour Press, 1996. This book is a combination of two of Turnbull's earlier works, *Samurai Warriors* and *Samurai Warlords: The Book of the Daimyo*. Featured are James Field's illustrations of samurai armor drawn from original sources.

H. Paul Varley, *Japanese Culture: A Short History*. Tokyo: Charles E. Tuttle, 1973. A concise but comprehensive source on Japanese culture.

Henry Wiencek, *The Lords of Japan*. Chicago: Stonehenge Press, 1982. Full-color photographs of Japanese art treasures and architectural marvels are presented along with stories of wealthy and powerful warlords who patronized the arts.

William Scott Wilson, trans., *Ideals of the Samurai: Writings of Japanese Warriors*. Burbank, CA: Ohara Publications, 1982. A collection of letters, documents, and treatises written by famous samurai warriors. A good source for primary materials.

Index

Picture Credits

Cover photo: Boston Museum of Fine Arts

AKG London, 22, 29, 35, 70, 71 (top), 81, 84, 89

Art Resource, NY, 47, 71

Corbis, 92

Corbis-Bettmann, 10, 12, 13, 15, 20, 21, 37, 43, 46, 72, 78, 85

Giraudon/Art Resource, NY, 48

© Erich Lessing/Art Resource, NY, 75

The Newark Museum/Art Resource, NY, 30, 65

North Wind Picture Archives, 23, 33, 63, 87

Reuters/Kimimasa Mayama/Archive Photos, 95

Scala/Art Resource, NY, 16 (right)

© Smithsonian Institution/Courtesy of the Freer Gallery of Art, 77

Stock Montage, Inc., 32, 34, 53, 58, 60, 74 (bottom), 91, 93

UPI/Corbis-Bettmann, 44

Werner Forman Archive/L.J. Anderson Collection/Art Resource, NY, 19

Werner Forman Archive/Art Institute of Chicago/Art Resource, NY, 40

Werner Forman Archive/Art Resource, NY, 14, 16 (left), 26, 27, 51, 56

Woodfin Camp & Associates, Inc., 61

About the Author

Eleanor J. Hall is a freelance writer who has had several careers. For many years she taught sociology and anthropology at a community college in southern Illinois. After retiring from teaching, she became an educational counselor in an Illinois prison for a time.

From 1988 to 1993, she worked as an interpreter of history, a museum specialist, and a writer for the National Park Service at the Gateway Arch in St. Louis. More recently, she has been a volunteer in various capacities for the U.S. Forest Service, the National Park Service, and several state parks.

While associated with the National Park Service, she wrote two curriculum guides that were distributed parkwide: *The Oregon Trail: Yesterday and Today* and *When Two Worlds Met: An Observance of the Columbus Quincentennial.*

Her current freelance work includes *The Lewis and Clark Expedition* and *Garbage* for Lucent Books. In addition she writes monthly children's activity columns and feature articles for various periodicals. She now lives, travels, and writes in the western United States.